STUDY GUIDE

Great Expectations

Charles Dickens

WITH CONNECTIONS

HOLT, RINEHART AND **WINSTON**

Harcourt Brace & Company

Austin • New York • Orlando • Atlanta • San Francisco • Boston • Dallas • Toronto • London

Staff Credits

Associate Director: Mescal Evler

Manager of Editorial Operations: Robert R. Hoyt

Managing Editor: Bill Wahlgren

Executive Editor: Emily Shenk

Editor: M. Kathleen Judge

Editorial Staff: *Assistant Managing Editor,* Marie H. Price; *Copyediting Manager,* Michael Neibergall; *Senior Copyeditor,* Mary Malone; *Copyeditors,* Joel Bourgeois, Gabrielle Field, Suzi A. Hunn, Jane M. Kominek, Millicent Ondras, Theresa Reding, Désirée Reid, Kathleen Scheiner; *Editorial Coordinators,* Jill O'Neal, Mark Holland, Marcus Johnson, Tracy DeMont; *Assistant Editorial Coordinators,* Summer Del Monte, Janet Riley; *Support Staff,* Lori De La Garza; *Word Processors,* Ruth Hooker, Margaret Sanchez, Kelly Keeley, Elizabeth Butler, Gail Coupland

Permissions: Lee Noble, Catherine Paré

Design: *Art Director, Book & Media Design,* Joe Melomo

Image Services: *Art Buyer Supervisor,* Elaine Tate

Prepress Production: Beth Prevelige, Simira Davis, Joan Lindsay

Manufacturing Coordinator: Michael Roche

Electronic Publishing (the Connections): *Senior Manager,* Carol Martin; *Administrative Coordinators,* Rina Ouellette, Sally Williams; *Operators,* JoAnn Brown, Lana Kaupp, Christopher Lucas

Cover Illustration: John Montelone

HRW is a registered trademark licensed to Holt, Rinehart and Winston.

Printed in the United States of America

ISBN 0-03-095756-7

23456 085 02 01

TABLE *of* CONTENTS

Using This Study Guide

Approaching the Novel

The successful study of a novel often depends on students' enthusiasm, curiosity, and openness. The ideas in **Introducing the Novel** will help you create such a climate for your class. Background information in **About the Writer** and **About the Novel** can also be used to pique students' interest.

Reading and Responding to the Novel

Making Meanings questions are designed for both individual response and group or class discussion. They range from personal response to high-level critical thinking.

Reading Strategies worksheets contain graphic organizers. They help students explore techniques that enhance both comprehension and literary analysis. Many worksheets are appropriate for more than one set of chapters.

Novel Notes provide high-interest information relating to historical, cultural, literary, and other elements of the novel. The **Investigate** questions and **Reader's Log** ideas guide students to further research and consideration.

Choices suggest a wide variety of activities for exploring different aspects of the novel, either individually or collaboratively. The results may be included in a portfolio or used as springboards for larger projects.

Glossary and Vocabulary (1) clarifies allusions and other references and (2) provides definitions students may refer to as they read. The **Vocabulary Worksheets** activities are based on the Vocabulary Words.

Reader's Log, Double-Entry Journal, and **Group Discussion Log** model formats and spark ideas for responding to the novel. These pages are designed to be a resource for independent reading as well.

Responding to the Novel as a Whole

The following features provide options for culminating activities that can be used in whole-class, small-group, or independent-study situations.

Novel Review provides a format for summarizing and integrating the major literary elements.

Novel Projects suggest multiple options for culminating activities. **Writing About the Novel, Cross-Curricular Connections,** and **Multimedia and Internet Connections** propose project options that extend the text into other genres, content areas, and environments.

Responding to the Connections

Making Meanings questions in **Exploring the Connections** facilitate discussion of the additional readings in the HRW LIBRARY edition of this novel.

This Study Guide is intended to

- *provide maximum versatility and flexibility*
- *serve as a ready resource for background information on both the author and the book*
- *act as a catalyst for discussion, analysis, interpretation, activities, and further research*
- *provide reproducible masters that can be used for either individual or collaborative work, including discussions and projects*
- *provide multiple options for evaluating students' progress through the novel and the Connections*

Literary Elements

- plot structure
- major themes
- characterization
- setting
- point of view
- symbolism, irony, and other elements appropriate to the title

Making Meanings Reproducible Masters

- First Thoughts
- Shaping Interpretations
- Connecting with the Text
- Extending the Text
- Challenging the Text

A **Reading Check** focuses on review and comprehension.

The Worksheets Reproducible Masters

- Reading Strategies Worksheets
- Literary Elements Worksheets
- Vocabulary Worksheets

Reaching All Students

Because the questions and activities in this Study Guide are in the form of reproducible masters, labels indicating the targeted types of learners have been omitted.

Most classrooms include students from a variety of backgrounds and with a range of learning styles. The questions and activities in this Study Guide have been developed to meet diverse student interests, abilities, and learning styles. Of course, students are full of surprises, and a question or activity that is challenging to an advanced student can also be handled successfully by students who are less proficient readers. The interest level, flexibility, and variety of these questions and activities make them appropriate for a range of students.

Struggling Readers and Students with Limited English Proficiency: The **Making Meanings** questions, the **Choices** activities, and the **Reading Strategies** worksheets all provide opportunities for students to check their understanding of the text and to review their reading. The **Novel Projects** ideas are designed for a range of student abilities and learning styles. Both questions and activities motivate and encourage students to make connections to their own interests and experiences. The **Vocabulary Worksheets** can be used to facilitate language acquisition. **Dialogue Journals,** with you the teacher or with more advanced students as respondents, can be especially helpful to these students.

Advanced Students: The writing opportunity suggested with the **Making Meanings** questions and the additional research suggestions in **Novel Notes** should offer a challenge to these students. The **Choices** and **Novel Projects** activities can be taken to advanced levels. **Dialogue Journals** allow advanced students to act as mentors or to engage each other intellectually.

Auditory Learners: A range of suggestions in this Study Guide targets students who respond particularly well to auditory stimuli: making and listening to audiotapes and engaging in class discussion, role-playing, debate, oral reading, and oral presentation. See **Making Meanings** questions, **Choices,** and **Novel Projects** options (especially **Cross-Curricular Connections** and **Multimedia and Internet Connections**).

Visual/Spatial Learners: Students are guided to create visual representations of text scenes and concepts and to analyze films or videos in **Choices** and in **Novel Projects.** The **Reading Strategies** and **Literary Elements Worksheets** utilize graphic organizers as a way to both assimilate and express information.

Tactile/Kinesthetic Learners: The numerous interactive, hands-on, and problem-solving projects are designed to encourage the involvement of students motivated by action and movement. The projects also provide an opportunity for **interpersonal learners** to connect with others through novel-related tasks. The **Group Discussion Log** will help students track the significant points of their interactions.

Verbal Learners: For students who naturally connect to the written and spoken word, the **Reader's Logs** and **Dialogue Journals** will have particular appeal. This Study Guide offers numerous writing opportunities: See **Making Meanings, Choices, Novel Notes,** and **Writing About the Novel** in **Novel Projects.** These options should also be attractive to **intrapersonal learners.**

Assessment Options

Perhaps the most important goal of assessment is to provide feedback on the effectiveness of instructional strategies. As you monitor the degree to which your students understand and engage with the novel, you will naturally adjust the frequency and ratio of class to small-group and verbal to nonverbal activities, as well as the extent to which direct teaching of reading strategies, literary elements, or vocabulary is appropriate to your students' needs.

If you are in an environment where **portfolios** contain only carefully chosen samples of students' writing, you may want to introduce a second, "working," portfolio and negotiate grades with students after examining all or selected items from this portfolio.

The features in this Study Guide are designed to facilitate a variety of assessment techniques.

Reader's Logs and Double-Entry Journals can be briefly reviewed and responded to (students may wish to indicate entries they would prefer to keep private). The logs and journals are an excellent measure of students' engagement with and understanding of the novel.

Group Discussion Log entries provide students with an opportunity for self-evaluation of their participation in both book discussions and project planning.

Making Meanings questions allow you to observe and evaluate a range of student responses. Those who have difficulty with literal and interpretive questions may respond more completely to **Connecting** and **Extending**. The **Writing Opportunity** provides you with the option of ongoing assessment: You can provide feedback to students' brief written responses to these prompts as they progress through the novel.

Reading Strategies Worksheets, Novel Review, and Literary Elements Worksheets lend themselves well to both quick assessment and students' self-evaluation. They can be completed collaboratively and the results shared with the class, or students can compare their individual responses in a small-group environment.

Choices activities and writing prompts offer all students the chance to successfully complete an activity, either individually or collaboratively, and share the results with the class. These items are ideal for peer evaluation and can help prepare students for presenting and evaluating larger projects at the completion of the novel unit.

Vocabulary Worksheets can be used as diagnostic tools or as part of a concluding test.

Novel Projects evaluations might be based on the degree of understanding of the novel demonstrated by the project. Students' presentations of their projects should be taken into account, and both self-evaluation and peer evaluation can enter into the overall assessment.

The **Test** is a traditional assessment tool in three parts: objective items, short-answer questions, and essay questions.

Questions for Self-evaluation and Goal Setting

- What are the three most important things I learned in my work with this novel?
- How will I follow up so that I remember them?
- What was the most difficult part of working with this novel?
- How did I deal with the difficulty, and what would I do differently?
- What two goals will I work toward in my reading, writing, group, and other work?
- What steps will I take to achieve those goals?

Items for a "Working" Portfolio

- reading records
- drafts of written work and project plans
- audio- and videotapes of presentations
- notes on discussions
- reminders of cooperative projects, such as planning and discussion notes
- artwork
- objects and mementos connected with themes and topics in the novel
- other evidence of engagement with the book

For help with establishing and maintaining portfolio assessment, examine the **Portfolio Management System** *in* ELEMENTS OF LITERATURE.

Answer Key

The Answer Key at the back of this guide is not intended to be definitive or to set up a right-wrong dichotomy. In questions that involve interpretation, however, students' responses should be defended by citations from the text.

More on Dickens

Hardwick, Michael and Mollie. **The Charles Dickens Encyclopedia.** Berkshire, England: Citadel Press, 1973.

Hornback, Bert G. **Great Expectations: A Novel of Friendship.** Boston: Twayne Publishers, 1987.

Kaplan, Fred. **Dickens: A Biography.** New York: William Morrow, 1988.

Page, Norman. **A Dickens Companion.** New York: Schocken Books, 1984.

Pool, Daniel. **What Jane Austen Ate and Charles Dickens Knew.** New York: Simon and Schuster, Inc., 1993.

Schlicke, Paul, ed. **Oxford Reader's Companion to Dickens.** Oxford: Oxford University Press, 1999.

Also by Dickens

Sketches by Boz (1836)

The Posthumous Papers of the Pickwick Club (1836–37)

Oliver Twist (1837–38)

Nicholas Nickleby (1838–39)

The Old Curiosity Shop (1841)

Martin Chuzzlewit (1843–44)

A Christmas Carol (1843)

David Copperfield (1849–50)

Bleak House (1852–53)

Hard Times (1854)

Little Dorrit (1855–57)

A Tale of Two Cities (1859)

Our Mutual Friend (1864–65)

The Letters of Charles Dickens (1938)

A biography of Charles Dickens appears in *Great Expectations, HRW LIBRARY edition.* You may wish to share this additional biographical information with your students.

Charles Dickens, the most enduringly popular and perhaps the greatest of Victorian novelists, was born near Portsmouth on the southern coast of England in 1812. His childhood included both happiness and horror—happiness because his father encouraged him to develop his talent for writing and acting, and horror because his father was thrown into debtors' prison. As was the custom at the time, the debtor's wife accompanied her husband and took along the younger children. The second eldest of the eight children, Charles, at age twelve, was sent to work at a shoepolish warehouse—twelve hours a day, six days a week—and was permitted to visit his family only on Sundays. Though a change of fortune rescued the family, this childhood experience haunted Dickens for the rest of his life. His hatred of social injustice and his sympathy for society's outcasts can be traced to these bitter memories.

Before he embarked on his career writing fiction, Dickens worked as a court reporter and a journalist. In 1836, at age twenty-four, he published *Sketches by Boz,* prose pieces about English life and manners. Seven weeks later he began publication of his first serial novel: *The Posthumous Papers of the Pickwick Club.* The first of twenty installments appeared on March 31, and two days later he married Catherine Hogarth, the daughter of a magazine editor.

Pickwick made Dickens famous, and he continued to publish most of his subsequent novels serially, often in magazines that he himself owned. This method of writing and publishing forced him to think ahead and to construct master plans to ensure continuity. In time, Dickens became an expert at weaving the intricate and suspenseful plots of his serials. In *Great Expectations,* the seams joining the installments remain largely invisible, and the work appears as an organic whole. With each new novel, Dickens's popularity grew, despite some critics who were convinced that anything so popular with the general public must be "vulgar," crude, and lacking refinement.

Needing to support an ever-growing family (he and Catherine had ten children), Dickens set off on a lecture tour of the United States in 1842. He used his lecture as a forum to advocate the abolition of slavery and the passage of international copyright laws to prevent the pirating of his novels. After his return to England, he published the novel *Martin Chuzzlewit* and, in December 1843, his perennially popular *A Christmas Carol.* A steady stream of novels followed—

About the Writer *(cont.)*

before his death he published fourteen novels and held several editorial positions at magazines. Dickens's unswerving devotion to his "imaginative life," however, strained the marriage, and he separated from his wife in 1858.

Dickens enjoyed a popularity and celebrity scarcely imaginable by an author today. In all of Europe and North America, no other writer was more widely read. Characters from *The Pickwick Papers and Nicholas Nickleby* were painted on clothing, dishes, and posters, and Dickens was in great demand as a speaker at literary societies, clubs, and fund-raisers. Although renowned for his novels, Dickens also left sparkling examples of his wit and passion in his many speeches, letters, journalism, travel writing, and notebooks.

Dickens continued to publish and lecture during the last decade of his life. In 1870, at the age of fifty-five, he again toured the United States, giving spirited public readings before enthusiastic audiences. He read so dramatically from his novels that people in the audience fainted, and *his* pulse rate would rise to dangerously high levels. The strain of the tour ruined his health. Retiring to his country home at Gad's Hill in Kent, he began his last novel, *The Mystery of Edwin Drood,* a detective story. Before unraveling the mystery surrounding the title character's disappearance, Dickens died suddenly from a stroke. After a private ceremony, Dickens was buried in the Poets' Corner of Westminster Abbey.

About the Novel

Special Considerations

Possible sensitive issues in this novel include differences between social classes, several antisemitic comments by minor characters and unflattering references to the Romany people (referred to as "Gypsies" in the novel) and people of African descent, and the intimidation, bullying, and abandonment of children.

For Viewing

Great Expectations. 1946, not rated. This is a classic version of Dickens's tale starring John Mills, Jean Simmons, and Alec Guinness.

Great Expectations. 1981. A five-hour BBC made-for-television production starring Gerry Sundquist as Pip.

Great Expectations. Twentieth Century Fox, 1998, rated R. This modern adaptation replaces London with New York City and blacksmithing with fishing; in its attempts to update and Americanize the story, the film strays from the original text. The film stars Gwyneth Paltrow, Ethan Hawke, Robert De Niro, and Anne Bancroft.

Great Expectations. Mobil Masterpiece Theater, 1999. A made-for-television production starring Ioan Gruffudd as Pip.

For Listening

Great Expectations. Audio Partners Publishing, 1998. A twelve-cassette, unabridged audio recording read by Martin Jarvis.

Great Expectations. Bantam Doubleday Dell Publishing, 1994. A four-cassette BBC Radio dramatization (abridged).

Historical Context

Just as Dickens contrasted working-class life with gentility, he contrasted the settings of his stories to provide another type of social commentary. He set *Great Expectations* in an unnamed rural village in Kent and in bustling London thirty miles away.

The novel begins in the early 1800s, a time when England was still coping with changes wrought by the Industrial Revolution. The invention of steam-powered machinery had led to the rapid development of factories and the demand for more labor. Improvements in farm tools and farming techniques had increased food production, giving rise to large farms and squeezing out thousands of small farmers who often fled to the overcrowded cities to work in factories under intolerable conditions for long hours at low pay. The increase in food supplies had stimulated population growth, expanding the number of workers and consumers, as well as a prosperous middle class of merchants, bankers, lawyers, and other professionals who had helped dilute the rigid class system composed of the very rich at the top and the very poor at the bottom.

Pip, the main character, lives in a village with his guardian, Joe Gargery. Joe, the village blacksmith, represents the warmth, honesty, and simplicity of rural life that was rapidly vanishing during this era. When Pip leaves the neat rural village for London, he is dismayed by his first impression of the city— "rather ugly, crooked, narrow, and dirty." London at the time of the novel was a bustling, prosperous city, the hub of an empire that stretched around the world. However, this London was not yet the modern Victorian city that it was in 1860 when Dickens was writing his novel. Trains had not yet replaced the horse and carriage as the chief mode of transportation. Steamships were still in their infancy. Raw sewage still flowed along London streets because underground sewers had not yet been built. Vast dilapidated slums for factory workers crowded along the Thames and offered a sharp contrast to the stately palaces and government buildings.

It is in a dismal London that Dickens places Pip during the second and third stages of his story. The unhealthy atmosphere is epitomized by the looming presence of Newgate Prison, a place made infamous by its appalling conditions and public executions. Here, an "exceedingly dirty and partially drunk minister of justice" offers to let Pip watch part of a trial, and then "he was so good as to take me into a yard and show me where the gallows was kept, and also where people were publicly whipped, and then he showed me the Debtors' Door, out of which culprits came to be hanged. . . . This was horrible, and gave me a sickening idea of London. . . ." This was a brutal society that prospered by condoning child labor in factories, encouraged crowds to gather at Newgate for public executions, and shipped criminals to Australia. Nevertheless, if a person had money, London could be entertaining and exciting; it was the seat of wealth and power, and anyone with "great expectations" lived there.

Literary Context

Victorian England participated in the transformation of English society. Writers in all genres responded to these changes by dramatizing and probing social problems, especially the wretched conditions of the lower classes, and by severely criticizing those who took advantage of the poor, particularly poor children. Charles Dickens had experienced such circumstances firsthand, and no one depicted the downtrodden with more compassion and sentiment, or explored the dehumanizing effects of greed, money, and "great expectations" on innumerable characters with more insight than Dickens.

In this regard, he follows a long line of writers such as Jonathan Swift, and two of Dickens's favorites, Henry Fielding and the Spanish novelist Miguel de Cervantes. As a child, Dickens also read works by Samuel Richardson, Oliver Goldsmith, Daniel Defoe, and Tobias Smollett. Most of these writers examined the human condition in rough-humored, sprawling narratives replete with unforgettable characters. They influenced Dickens greatly, but Shakespeare influenced him most of all: "An event that stuck in his memory, that he wrote about years afterward as a defining myth, brought father and son past an imposing late eighteenth-century house on the Gravesend Road called Gad's Hill Place, the hill associated with Falstaff's adventures in Shakespeare's *Henry IV.* To the small boy, used to his lower-middle-class world and the cramped houses of his earlier childhood, it seemed a palatial wonder. If he 'were to be very persevering and were to work hard,' his father

told him, he 'might some day come to live in it.' [Dickens later bought the house.] The association of Shakespeare, his favorite author, with success; his father's encouragement to think nothing impossible for the assiduous and the talented; and the association of writing with money and status, all must have produced feelings and connections that had a strong influence on him" (Fred Kaplan, *Dickens: A Biography*). Appropriately it is with William Shakespeare that Dickens is most often compared, especially for sheer inventiveness and characterization. However, his early writing—*Sketches By Boz,* humorous personal impressions of everyday English life—also owes much to writers such as Leigh Hunt and Tobias Smollett.

To reach readers, Dickens used the most popular literary form of his time—the novel. Dickens and his publishers favored serial publication of his novels as a way to heighten reader anticipation and increase sales. Despite scheduling and deadline demands, it gave Dickens the opportunity to do what he did best, create characters and suspenseful events. (*The Pickwick Papers* has some 300 characters.) As literary critic Alan Shelston notes, serial publication "also had the effect of intensifying the relationship between the author and his audience to a degree that can perhaps be compared with the oral narrative poem or the Elizabethan stage." Readers in the United States would wait at docks for incoming English ships and yell questions to crews about the fate of particular Dickens characters in the serials.

Quote from *Dickens: A Biography* by Fred Kaplan. Copyright © 1988 by Fred Kaplan. Originally published by William Morrow , New York, 1988. Reprinted by permission of **Georges Borchardt, Inc. on behalf of the author.**

Later in his life, with the novels *David Copperfield* and *Great Expectations,* Dickens contributed to the coming-of-age genre. German writer Johann Wolfgang von Goethe had fathered the genre of *Bildungsroman* (a German word meaning novel of education) with *Wilhelm Meister's Apprenticeship* (1795–1796). Other authors who have contributed to this genre include James Joyce with *A Portrait of the Artist as a Young Man* (1916) and J. D. Salinger with *Catcher in the Rye* (1951).

Critical Responses

For a while after his death, Dickens's reputation was challenged. Critics accused him of being sentimental and melodramatic, and of creating improbable plots that often depended on coincidence. Many considered him a writer far inferior to Tolstoy and Dostoyevsky. These two giants themselves, however, readily admitted Dickens's greatness. Tolstoy claimed that "all his characters are my personal friends." In this century, few dispute that Dickens is one of the pre-eminent writers of all time. George Orwell, in *Dickens, Dali & Others,* calls him "an institution that there is no getting away from." He adds, "I should not doubt whether anyone who has actually read Dickens can go a week without remembering him in one context or another. Whether you approve of him or not, he is there, like the Nelson Column."

Like all of Dickens's other novels, *Great Expectations* has been the subject of criticism since its original publication. Some of it has been unfavorable, like the following excerpt from a review that appeared in *Blackwood's Magazine* in 1862:

> So far as *Great Expectations* is a sensation novel, it occupies itself with incidents all but impossible, and in themselves strange, dangerous and exciting; but so far as it is one of the series of Mr. Dickens's works, it is feeble, fatigued and colourless. One feels that he must have got tired of it as the work went on, and that the creatures he had called into being, but who are no longer the lively men and women they used to be, must have bored him unspeakably before it was time to cut short their career, and throw a hasty and impatient hint of their future to stop the tiresome public appetite.
>
>   —from "Sensation Novels,"
>   Margaret Oliphant

Most of the reviews of *Great Expectations* have been highly favorable. G. Robert Strange summarizes the elements that make *Great Expectations* a masterpiece:

> *Great Expectations* . . . demonstrates the subtlety of Dickens's art; it displays a consistent control of narrative, imagery, and theme which gives meaning to the stark outline of the fable, and the symbolic weight to every character and detail. It proves Dickens's ability (which has frequently been denied) to combine his genius for comedy with his fictional presentation of some of the most serious and permanently interesting of human concerns.
>
>   —from "Expectations Well Lost: Dickens's
>   Fable for His Time,"G. Robert Strange

The Novel at a Glance

Plot and Setting

Great Expectations's **first-person narrator,** the adult Pip, relates his life story from the age of seven to the age of thirty-five. The novel is divided into three life stages (Chapters 1–19, Chapters 20–39, and Chapters 40–59). The setting, in early nineteenth-century England, alternates between a peaceful rural village and a crowded, hectic London.

A **Literary Elements Worksheet** focusing on **atmosphere** appears on page 56 of this Study Guide.

Novel Genre

Great Expectations can be described as both a ***Bildungsroman*** and a **moral fairy tale.**

Bildungsroman is a German word for novels of education or maturation. Such a novel depicts the education or spiritual growth of the main character as he or she undergoes a moral crisis. *Great Expectations* follows Pip through the various stages of a journey— not merely a life's journey from childhood to adulthood but also a spiritual journey through the stages of innocence, sin, and redemption.

A **moral fairy tale** is a story that teaches an important lesson and contains whimsical and grotesque elements also common in childhood stories. In the case of *Great Expectations,* Miss Havisham is like a gingerbread-house witch who devours children, and Estella is the beautiful princess. Wemmick lives in a fairy-tale castle, and Pip's good fortune is like a wish that has been magically fulfilled. By drawing on the conventions of children's literature, Dickens allows his audience to view his fictional world through a child's eyes.

A **Literary Elements Worksheet** focusing on ***Bildungsroman*** appears on page 59 of this Study Guide.

A **Literary Elements Worksheet** focusing on **moral fairy tale** appears on page 60 of this Study Guide.

Major Characters

Pip is the narrator and protagonist. Pip (Philip Pirrip) begins the story of his life as a seven-year-old orphan and progresses through his desire for greater social status. When he pursues his "great expectations," he learns the true meaning of being a gentleman.

Joe Gargery is Pip's caretaker and brother-in-law. Joe is an uneducated blacksmith with a good heart. Joe sees Pip as his equal or better and never begrudges Pip wealth or status.

Mrs. Joe Gargery is Pip's sister and guardian. She has a bad temper and shows little love for Pip or Joe. After an attack which leaves her maimed and helpless, her character softens.

Abel Magwitch is a convict whom Pip helps, but it is later revealed that Magwitch is also Pip's benefactor. Living in exile, he has made an honest living to provide for Pip.

Miss Havisham is a wealthy, bitter spinster who lives at Satis House.

For most of the novel, Pip believes Miss Havisham to be his anonymous benefactor, and she does nothing to disabuse him.

Estella Havisham is a contemporary of Pip and the strikingly beautiful yet cruel adopted daughter of Miss Havisham. A fascination with Estella is at the crux of Pip's inner conflict throughout the novel.

Mr. Jaggers is Pip's guardian in London and a criminal lawyer. He manages Miss Havisham's affairs and is Magwitch's lawyer.

Herbert Pocket is Pip's compassionate friend, the son of Pip's tutor, and Pip's roommate.

Themes

Great expectations: The words *great expectations* suggest future wealth or advancement. Pip looks forward to being wealthy, attaining a higher social position, and marrying Estella. Dickens structures his novel so that stage one deals with anticipating great expectations; stage two shows characters achieving their expectations with ironic results; and stage three reveals the folly of these expectations and how little lasting happiness they provide.

Love / friendship: The redemptive power of selfless love plays a central role in the novel. Each character searching for wealth and status actually longs for love. Pip, Miss Havisham, Magwitch, and Estella lack love and cannot be happy. Biddy and Joe lack wealth and status but have selfless love that they give unconditionally.

Appearance versus reality: In *Great Expectations,* appearances often do not reflect reality. Characters may appear to be something which they are not; both virtues and vices may be obscured.

The influence of the past on the present: The coincidences which propel Pip's story are frequently a result of the profound effect that the past has on the present. His expectations are the result of his act of kindness as a young boy, and his life is shaped by the decisions that Magwitch, Molly, Miss Havisham, and Jaggers made before he was born.

Irony: Time and again, outcomes in *Great Expectations* are different from what characters have expected. For example, Pip thinks that Miss Havisham is his benefactor; instead, Magwitch is. Irony emphasizes the theme of **appearance and reality** and suggests that life is often unpredictable and unfair.

A **Literary Elements Worksheet** focusing on **theme** appears on page 57 of this Study Guide.

Connecting with
ELEMENTS OF LITERATURE
You can use *Great Expectations* to extend students' explorations of the themes and topics presented in *Elements of Literature.*

• *Sixth Course:* The Victorian Period

Options

Engaging Issues

The issues raised in Great Expectations *continue to be both relevant and controversial. Use this activity to engage students in grappling with these issues which might affect their own lives.*

1. Create a five- to ten-question Dilemma Survey to introduce some of these issues. Students can survey one another or other members of the school community.

Possible topic with sample questions

Expectations

* Whose expectations of you affect your expectations for yourself? Are you more likely to feel ashamed or uncomfortable because of a derogatory comment from a teacher, a sibling, a member of the opposite sex, or your friend?

* Everyone has expectations. You may expect to play a professional sport, make a record, write a novel, attend Harvard, get married, travel to Africa, or any number of other things. Do you think you will be a failure in your own eyes if, in fifteen years, you have not succeeded in reaching your goal?

* While you are answering a question in class, students begin to snicker. You realize it is because of the way you said something: Your accent or your phrasing struck them as funny. Would you change your style of speech?

* When you are of a marrying age, what type of person would your parents be thrilled to see you marry? Why do you suppose that is?

2. Place students in small groups. Then, ask students to reach conclusions about what significantly influences people's expectations. Groups should then present their conclusions to the class, citing survey responses in support of their opinions.

READING / GROUP DISCUSSION

Humor, Hope, Horror

Read aloud to students the first four paragraphs of *Great Expectations*. Then, place students in groups of three. Ask one group member to look for the humor in the passage, one to illustrate the symbol of hope in the passage, and one to identify the horror. After they have had a few minutes to discuss these elements in small groups, discuss the elements as a class.

Introduce students to Dickens's style of humor that is often achieved through sophisticated wording, his symbolism through natural elements (Pip is in the marsh, but the marshes lead to a river, which runs to the open sea), and finally the brutality of the characters who will populate Pip's life.

ART / COLLAGE

A Picture of the Future

Provide students with magazines, calendars, and newspapers, and ask that they make two small collages. One collection of images is to represent *who* they want to be in fifteen years (character/personality traits), and the other collection of images is to represent *what* they want to be in fifteen years (occupation).

After students have finished, have them write on the back or bottom of their collages what the pictures and words represent. Then, ask students which would disappoint them more: to fall short of becoming *who* they want to be or to fall short of becoming *what* they want to be. Students should explain their responses in a paragraph or personal essay.

Chapters 1–9

Plot Synopsis

In the cemetery at the edge of a marsh where his parents are buried, seven-year-old Pip encounters an escaped convict in a leg iron. The man threatens to kill the boy unless he returns the next morning with food and a file. Terrified, Pip goes home to the house where he lives with his sister, Mrs. Joe, and her husband, Joe Gargery, the village blacksmith. Before dawn, Pip steals food from his sister's pantry and the file from Joe's forge and runs back to the marshes. There he spots a second convict in the mist but soon finds "the right man," who becomes agitated when he learns of another convict's presence.

During the Gargerys' Christmas celebration later that day, guilt-ridden Pip fears that his sister will discover his theft. Just as she is about to find that food is missing, soldiers arrive at the door with a set of broken handcuffs and request a blacksmith. While Joe repairs the cuffs for the sergeant, the group learns that the soldiers are hunting two escaped convicts. Joe and Pip join the pursuit.

The search party finds the convicts bloody from fighting each other, and both men are apprehended. To protect the boy who helped him, Pip's convict confesses to stealing the food and the file. Though relieved of blame, Pip continues to feel guilty and fears losing Joe's confidence if Joe ever learns of the deception.

A year later, Pip and Joe are at home discussing Pip's efforts at writing. Though he is struggling to learn to read and write, Pip expects to become Joe's apprentice when he is old enough. When Pip asks about Joe's education, he discovers that Joe is illiterate. The blacksmith describes how his father kept him away from school and forced him to work at an early age. He asks Pip to overlook these shortcomings. Joe's tender simplicity and obvious respect for Pip cause the boy to have "new admiration" for Joe. Joe's pompous and hypocritical uncle, Mr.

Pumblechook, arrives with the news that he has arranged to take Pip to Miss Havisham, an "immensely rich and grim lady," who wants a boy to come and play at her house. Mrs. Joe suggests that "this boy's future may be made by his going to Miss Havisham's."

At Satis House, Miss Havisham's decaying mansion, Pip meets a girl named Estella. Estella is very pretty, very proud, self-possessed, and scornful of young Pip. Miss Havisham, wearing a faded and yellowed bridal dress, is old and withered, like "some ghastly waxwork." The curtains in her room are perpetually drawn to block out all sunlight, and every clock has been stopped at twenty minutes to nine. Pip is ordered to play cards with Estella, who disdainfully objects and calls him "a stupid, clumsy labouring-boy." Hurt by her criticism, Pip looks upon his coarse hands and common boots as "vulgar appendages" and wishes that he had been "more genteelly brought up."

Back home, Pip fabricates a fanciful tale for his sister and Mr. Pumblechook of all the "marvels" he saw at Miss Havisham's. The two agree that Miss Havisham will "do something" for the boy. However, Pip tells the truth to Joe and confesses how miserable he feels at being "ignorant and backward." Joe tries to comfort the boy and encourages him to continue his studies, but Pip realizes his experience at Satis House has "made great changes" in him.

Literary Elements

Dickens sets the stage for his moral tale by introducing major **characters** who will influence Pip's growth: Joe, who embodies warmth and selfless love; the convict Magwitch, who will twice alter Pip's destiny; Miss Havisham, who represents the damage caused by the inability to adjust to failed or disappointed expectations; and Estella, who remains the object of Pip's romantic delusions and the source of his self-loathing. Dickens also introduces three **settings** that represent the conflicting forces shaping Pip's development: the gloomy marshes where Pip first becomes aware of the world's evils; his unpleasant home with the ill-tempered Mrs. Joe and the good-natured Joe; and Miss Havisham's dismal, decaying house with the cold Estella.

Pip's circumstances evoke sympathy. **First-person point of view** establishes **inner conflict** between innocence and experience. The disparity between the tone of the well-educated, adult narrator and the confused child creates a comic voice that lightens the story.

Symbolism

Pip's very name is a symbol. A *pip* is a seed, that which will grow and flourish.

In a **Bildungsroman** such as *Great Expectations,* it is characteristic for the main character to undergo a moral crisis while encountering characters representing various attitudes toward life.

- Mrs. Joe's coarse and impregnable physical appearance mirrors her coarse and impregnable temperament: She had "such a prevailing redness of skin that I sometimes used to wonder whether it was possible she washed herself with a nutmeg-grater instead of soap."
- Joe, on the other hand, embodies simplicity, honesty, compassion, and warmth. He is a blacksmith, he always sits by the hearth, and he is always warm to his friend Pip.
- Magwitch, a social outcast, symbolizes something that Pip probably fears he will become. When Pip asks his sister about the prison ships called Hulks,

his sister cruelly informs him that "People are put in the Hulks because they murder, and because they rob, and forge, and do all sorts of bad; and they always begin by asking questions."
- Miss Havisham has removed herself from society because of a broken heart, but she at this point symbolizes, for Pip, a higher social position.
- Miss Havisham's adopted daughter, the beautiful but scornful Estella, embodies the contrast between **appearance and behavior.**

Themes: Mrs. Joe foreshadows Pip's **great expectations** when she says: "[T]his boy's fortune may be made by his going to Miss Havisham's." There, **ironically,** Pip is made to feel ashamed of his clothes and manners by Estella. Pip has begun to lose his innocence and to sense wrongly that wealth is the means to fulfill great expectations and an end in itself.

In these chapters, characters reveal **love** in greatly different ways. Joe's love is tender and unconditional. He remains loyal and understanding even when Mrs. Joe goes on her rampages. Mrs. Joe expresses her love through harsh discipline and control, ever believing that she is doing the right thing for Pip as she brings him up "by hand."

Such conflicting character traits are a dimension of **appearance versus reality.** The harsh convict who threatens Pip later conceals Pip's involvement in providing him with food, taking responsibility for the theft himself. Pip substitutes appearance for reality when, not wanting to describe Miss Havisham as she really is, he makes up a fabulous story about what he did at Satis House.

Chapters 10–19

Plot Synopsis

Hoping to become "uncommon," Pip asks Biddy, his schoolteacher's granddaughter, to tutor him. Afterward, at the local tavern with Joe, Pip sees a man who scares him by pointedly stirring his drink

with Joe's stolen file. The man gives Pip a shilling, which Mrs. Joe later discovers has been wrapped in two one-pound notes. Pip has a nightmare about the file and dreads that it will reappear when he least expects it.

At Satis House, Pip encounters some of Miss Havisham's unpleasant relatives and is slapped in the face by Estella as she escorts him upstairs. In a vermin-infested room, Miss Havisham points out her molding wedding cake and explains that she will be laid out in that room when she is dead. Later, in the garden, Pip is accosted by a "pale young gentleman" who exuberantly challenges Pip to a fight by butting him in the stomach. With each punch, Pip succeeds in knocking the boy down. Delighted by the fight between the boys, Estella allows the victor to kiss her on the cheek—a reward that Pip considers "worth nothing." For about ten months, Pip returns every other day to Satis House, where he pushes Miss Havisham around her rooms in a wheelchair and plays cards with Estella, who by turns is coldly tolerant, condescending, familiar, or hateful toward him. When Pip expresses a desire for learning, Miss Havisham offers no help. Instead, she seems to prefer Pip's ignorance. Then, realizing one day that Pip has grown taller, Miss Havisham announces that she thinks Pip should be apprenticed at once and asks for Joe to come to Satis House with Pip's indentures.

Awkwardly dressed in his Sunday best, Joe accompanies Pip to Satis House. Too intimidated to speak directly to Miss Havisham, Joe addresses his replies to her questions to Pip instead—much to the boy's embarrassment. Miss Havisham presents Pip with twenty-five guineas and says that his services will no longer be needed: "Gargery is your master now." Later, a reluctant guest at a family celebration in honor of his apprenticeship, Pip realizes that he will "never like Joe's trade." During his apprenticeship, Pip becomes increasingly ashamed of his home. He lives in constant fear that Estella might see him at the forge when his face and hands are dirty.

A year later Pip, with the secret intention of seeing Estella, asks Joe for a half-holiday to visit Miss Havisham. When Joe reluctantly allows this, his journeyman, Orlick, also demands time off. When Joe gives in, Mrs. Joe becomes enraged and argues bitterly with Orlick. At Satis House, Pip learns that Estella is abroad, and he leaves more dissatisfied than ever before. On his way home, Pip encounters Orlick, and they discuss the cannons which signal the escape of convicts from the prison ships. In the village, Pip discovers that his sister has been struck senseless in the kitchen of their house by someone wielding a filed leg iron.

Mrs. Joe remains an invalid, barely able to communicate. An escaped convict is the rumored culprit, but Pip suspects Orlick or the strange man with Joe's file. Biddy eventually moves in to care for Mrs. Joe and run the household. When Orlick is brought before Mrs. Joe, she acts kindly toward him, and so the mystery surrounding her assault remains unsolved.

For the next several years, Pip visits Miss Havisham on his birthday and each time receives a guinea as a present. Estella remains abroad, and nothing in the gloomy house seems to change. The place bewilders Pip, who continues to hate his trade and be ashamed of his home. He struggles to educate himself and one day confides to Biddy that he wants to be a gentleman because of his admiration for Estella and her superior gentility. Biddy, whom Pip considers "rather an extraordinary girl," says that if Pip wants to become a gentleman out of spite, then he had better ignore Estella's derision of him, and that if he must become a gentleman to win her over, then she is not worth having. Pip sees the wisdom in Biddy's words, but he continues to be driven by a madness in his heart for Estella, and he resists the bonds of affection between himself and Biddy. Secretly he hopes that Miss Havisham will make his fortune when his apprenticeship is complete.

In the fourth year of his apprenticeship, Pip and Joe are visited by Mr. Jaggers, a lawyer whom Pip had once seen at Satis House. He announces that Pip has an anonymous benefactor who intends to see Pip "come into a handsome property" and brought up as a gentleman "of great expectations," under the conditions that Pip always bear the name of Pip, that he not try to discover the identity of his benefactor, and that he move to London to be better educated. Mr. Jaggers, who will be Pip's new guardian, proposes that Pip be tutored by Matthew Pocket, a relation of Miss Havisham, and gives Pip money to buy clothes more suited to his new status. When Mr. Jaggers offers Joe money to compensate for the loss of Pip's services, the blacksmith breaks down and stammers that money cannot compensate for the loss of a friend. Pip, secretly convinced and delighted that Miss Havisham is his benefactor, is eager to begin his new life, but nevertheless feels vaguely dissatisfied with himself and lonelier than ever before.

Pip now looks upon his surroundings with an air of condescension. He wishes Joe were educated and well-mannered and thus "better qualified for a rise in station." When Pip confides this sentiment to Biddy, she is annoyed and replies that Joe "may be too proud to let any one take him out of a place that he is competent to fill, and fills well and with respect." Pip accuses Biddy of being envious of his rise in fortune. The next day, Pip is treated obsequiously by the clothiers and Mr. Pumblechook. Dressed in his new clothes, Pip bids farewell to Miss Havisham, whose seemingly intimate knowledge of the details of his good fortune further convinces Pip that she is his "fairy godmother." The next morning, too ashamed to be seen in his new clothes alongside Joe, Pip leaves alone for the coach to London. Once on board, aware of his ingratitude, Pip considers going back for a better parting, but hesitates until it is too late. Pip notes, "I went on. And the mists had all solemnly risen now, and the world lay spread before me."

Literary Elements

Novel Structure: Chapter 19 concludes the first stage of Pip's expectations and the **exposition** of the plot.

Characterization: These chapters chart the rise of Pip's dissatisfaction with himself, his home, his position in life, and his family. Once he is seduced by the charms of Satis House, Pip's dissatisfaction begins to flourish but does not bear its inevitable fruit—pride—until Jaggers's announcement of Pip's "great expectations." Pip begins to treat Joe and Biddy with condescension and contempt and chafes under Joe's selfless love. He exchanges the spiritual values of his childhood as embodied in Joe for the "genteel" material values of Miss Havisham.

Themes: The man with Joe's file reminds Pip of the criminal on the marshes, suggesting that the **past will continue to influence the present.** When Jaggers reveals that Pip has an anonymous benefactor, from Pip's perspective Miss Havisham **appears** to be this patron. Her actions do not dissuade him. Jaggers says that Pip has **great expectations** and will "be brought up as a gentleman." Blinded by obsessive **love** for Estella, Pip believes that by becoming a gentleman he will be worthy of her. By contrast, Joe's selfless **love** insulates him from false pride, self-deception, and the desire for wealth and status.

Foreshadowing

- In Chapter 17, Biddy's advice to Pip that Estella may not be worth winning if he must change so drastically foreshadows the nature of his relationship to Estella.
- The leg iron used in the attack on Mrs. Joe and the man with the file foreshadow Pip's continuing bond with the convict. When Mrs. Joe is assaulted with a filed leg iron, the incident renews the guilty feelings that Pip had as a child.

Symbolism: *Satis* is the root for the word *satisfaction.* **Ironically,** Satis House has become a monument to Miss Havisham's disappointment, and it only encourages dissatisfaction in Pip.

Chapters 20–35

Plot Synopsis

When Pip arrives in London, he is disappointed with the appearance of the city, but he is fascinated by the novelty of his experiences. He learns that Jaggers, his guardian, is a criminal lawyer of great expertise and power. Jaggers instructs Pip to go to young Mr. Pocket's rooms at Barnard's Inn where he will live, and then gives Pip a generous allowance. At Barnard's Inn—a dismal, dilapidated, rotting place— Pip is dismayed by the imperfection of the first of his great expectations. When Pip meets good-humored Herbert Pocket, they take to each other immediately. Pip is startled and amused to discover that Herbert is the boy with whom he once fought in Miss Havisham's garden.

Pip learns that Herbert had been summoned to Miss Havisham's that day to see if he would be a suitable fiancé for Estella, but Miss Havisham did not take a fancy to him. Herbert expresses relief and explains that Miss Havisham adopted Estella and brought her up "to wreak revenge on all the male sex" on account of the injury done to her by her fiancé. Herbert explains that by scheming with Miss Havisham's half-brother, Miss Havisham's fiancé bilked her of large sums of money and then failed to arrive for the wedding.

Herbert also explains that he works in a counting-house where he is paid nothing; nevertheless, he has great plans to become an insurer of ships. At Herbert's parents' house, Pip meets Herbert's family, including his proud but domestically helpless mother and his father, Matthew Pocket, who is to become Pip's tutor. At the Pockets' home, where he has an additional room, Pip meets fellow students Drummle, "a sulky kind of fellow," and Startop. From Mr. Pocket, Pip learns that his benefactor does not intend for him to be educated for a particular profession but rather to be a gentleman. Later, at Mr. Jaggers's offices, Pip becomes acquainted with the law clerk Wemmick, who tells Pip to observe carefully Mr. Jaggers's housekeeper, "a wild beast tamed."

One evening Pip accepts an invitation to dinner at Wemmick's house, a small replica of a Gothic castle. There Pip meets Wemmick's father and enjoys Wemmick's hospitality. The next morning Pip notes how Wemmick grows "dryer and harder" as they walk together toward Mr. Jaggers's offices. Mr. Jaggers invites Pip and his fellow students to dine with him. Jaggers's home, in contrast to Wemmick's, is stately but gloomy. Jaggers takes a curious interest in the boastful Drummle, whom Jaggers calls "one of the true sort," implying a criminal nature. During dinner, Pip notices the housekeeper, whose face reminds Pip of the faces conjured up by the witches in *Macbeth*. Jaggers forcefully bares Molly's wrists to prove that her hands are very powerful. Pip notices that one wrist is deeply scarred. In parting, Jaggers warns Pip to keep clear of Drummle.

When Pip receives a letter from Biddy saying that Joe plans to visit him in London, Pip begins to dread Joe's arrival. While they breakfast together, Joe, awkward and ill at ease, calls the impatient and intolerant Pip "sir." Joe bears a message from Miss Havisham that Estella is home and would like to see Pip. The next day Pip travels to his hometown, intending at first to stay with Joe, then deciding to stay at an inn. Pip shares the coach with two convicts and recognizes one of them as the man who had Joe's file and gave Pip two one-pound notes. Pip trembles with dread when he overhears that "his convict" had instigated that mysterious encounter years ago to thank Pip for having aided him. In town, Pip discovers that Mr. Pumblechook has told everyone that he has been Pip's patron, taking credit for grooming Pip so that he could be noticed by a wealthy benefactor.

Convinced that Miss Havisham is his benefactor and intends for him to restore Satis House and to marry Estella, whom he admits he loves "against reason," Pip sets off to visit them. At Satis House, Pip is admitted by Orlick, who is serving as gatekeeper. Pip at first does not recognize Estella, now a beautiful woman, but still as cold, proud, and willful as ever. Estella galvanizes Pip's decision to stay away from Joe and the forge. She then warns the admiring Pip that her heart is entirely without sympathy or sentiment, but Pip refuses to heed her. Estella's appearance strongly reminds Pip of someone, but he cannot recall who. Back in Miss Havisham's room, the grave lady repeatedly commands Pip to love Estella even "[i]f she tears your heart to pieces."

The next morning at the inn, Pip advises Mr. Jaggers (who had been to Satis House on business) to fire Orlick. Back in London and feeling guilty that he did not visit Joe, Pip sends a "penitential codfish and barrel of oysters," and confesses to Herbert not only his love and adoration for Estella but also his uneasiness at not knowing for certain what his benefactor's expectations for him actually are. Herbert soothes Pip's anxiety but frankly questions his attachment to Estella, as having her would "lead to miserable things." Pip agrees but says he cannot possibly "detach" himself from her. Herbert then confesses that he is secretly engaged but cannot marry until he is established in a profession.

Estella sends Pip a note announcing that she will arrive in London in two days and that she understands he will be meeting her coach. Arriving early at the coach-office, Pip encounters Wemmick. Pip and Wemmick go to Newgate Prison where Wemmick meets with a client. Pip muses about all the contacts he has had with the criminal element since childhood. His mind is on this when he meets Estella; seeing her face, he is struck again by the similarity between her and some "nameless shadow."

Estella tells Pip that she will be living in London with a lady who will introduce her to society. She then admits how painful her childhood was, not because of Miss Havisham, but because of Miss Havisham's venal relations who now hate Pip and try

to put him out of favor with the woman they too believe is his benefactor. After reminding him that she has warned him against loving her, Estella allows Pip to kiss her cheek a second time. Pip escorts Estella to her residence and is told to visit when he wishes.

Torn between his expectations and a longing to return to a happier life with Joe, Biddy, and the honest work at the forge, Pip lives in a state of "chronic uneasiness"—compounded by an awareness that his expensive habits have put both him and Herbert into debt. One evening Pip receives a letter requesting his presence at his sister's funeral. Returning home, Pip's memories of having suffered at his sister's hands are softened. After the burial, Pip enjoys Joe's company and later walks with Biddy, who addresses him as "Mr. Pip." She explains the particulars of Pip's sister's death, notes that Orlick (who now works in the quarries) has been lurking about the forge, and expresses her admiration for Joe. Pip promises to visit Joe often—a promise that Biddy predicts will never be kept. Before parting the next day, Pip repeats his promise to Joe. As he walks away from the forge he admits to himself that Biddy was right: He has no real intention of ever returning.

Literary Elements

The mastery with which Dickens interweaves the elements of **setting, characterization,** and **plot** is particularly evident in Chapter 32, the scene in which Pip visits Newgate while waiting for Estella's arrival in London. Newgate epitomizes the pervading atmosphere of Pip's new environment; dismal and dirty like the rest of the city, it encompasses and "contaminates" Pip and reminds him of his many links with prison and crime. As Pip muses that this "stain" colors his fortune and advancement, he is struck by the absolute contrast in his mind between Newgate and Estella. When finally she appears, Pip is momentarily startled by the "nameless shadow" that he sees in her features. This nameless shadow is a **foreshadowing** of Estella's own stain and links with prison and crime.

Themes: Ironically, Pip's **great expectations** have brought him unhappiness. He lives an aimless life, incurs debt, feels guilt over his snubbing of Joe and Biddy, and experiences "chronic uneasiness." He has moments of clarity when he realizes that he probably would have been happier with Joe and Biddy, but his obsessive, unrequited **love** for Estella keeps him trapped in his genteel position. Unable to distinguish **appearance from reality,** Pip persists in his belief that Miss Havisham is his benefactor and remains confident that she intends for him to marry Estella and restore Satis House. The **past continues to exert its unsettling influence on the present.** Pip learns that "his convict" is the source of the two one-pound notes from the man with the file.

Chapters 36–48

Plot Synopsis

On his twenty-first birthday, Pip learns that he is to receive a yearly allowance with which he is to manage his own financial affairs until his benefactor comes forward. When Pip asks when that day will be, Mr. Jaggers says he does not know and does not want to know lest he be compromised.

Pip seeks advice from Wemmick about secretly helping to establish Herbert in business. Wemmick puts Pip in touch with a shipping broker who agrees to hire Herbert and eventually make him a partner in exchange for regular payments from Pip. Pip is pleased that his "expectations had done some good to somebody."

Pip's obsessive love for Estella grows although he is tortured to see her favor other suitors over him. One day she and Pip visit Miss Havisham. At Satis House, Pip notices that Miss Havisham dwells upon the details of Estella's romantic conquests. Although Pip now understands Miss Havisham's plans for Estella to make men miserable, he is still convinced that Miss Havisham will someday allow Estella to be his. When Estella extricates herself from Miss Havisham's embraces, the old lady accuses her of having a cold heart. Estella replies that she is incapable of giving what she never received (love), and that she is only as proud and hard as Miss Havisham has taught her to be. On hearing this Miss Havisham sinks to the floor in agony. Back in London, Pip is enraged to learn that Estella has been allowing Drummle to court her. Estella tells Pip that she deceives every suitor but him.

One stormy night when Pip is twenty-three, he is visited by a balding, elderly man—"his convict." He tells Pip of his undying gratitude, but Pip recoils, haughtily saying that thanks are not necessary. He then tries to sever their connection by repaying the man's gift of two one-pound notes, which the convict takes and burns. He explains that after being transported to Australia he made a fortune as a sheep farmer. He then reveals that he is Pip's benefactor. Pip is dumbfounded and horrified. When the convict explains that he would be hanged if anyone knew he had returned to England, Pip begins to fear for the man's safety. Pip grows despondent, realizing that Miss Havisham has merely used him in her plans of revenge. However, the sharpest pain comes with the realization that he has deserted Joe for these "great expectations" and can never undo the harm he has done.

In the morning, Pip stumbles over a man in the outer staircase, who quickly disappears. Pip learns that his visitor—whom he is calling his uncle—has been followed. The convict, actually named Abel Magwitch, tells Pip that he intends to stay in England because he wants to lavish more money on Pip and to have the pleasure of observing the gentleman he has created. Pip secures nearby lodging for his "uncle," and they agree that he will disguise himself as Mr. Provis, a prosperous farmer. Magwitch still seems like a felon, and Pip still recoils from him. Soon, Herbert is sworn to keep Magwitch's secret as well.

It dawns on Pip that he has caused the danger to Magwitch's life and is therefore responsible for his safety. Pip determines that he must get Magwitch out of England and decides that he can no longer accept money from Magwitch.

The next day Magwitch tells Pip and Herbert about his life. Deserted as a child, he stole food to survive and grew up as a drifter until he fell in with a "gentleman" named Compeyson. Magwitch recounts how another associate of Compeyson, named Arthur, died in a fit of delirium, after which Magwitch became Compeyson's "slave" in crime. Eventually, both were arrested and tried. Magwitch was defended by Jaggers, but Compeyson's lawyer shifted the blame from the young "gentleman" to his older accomplice, who already had a criminal record. When Magwitch was sentenced to fourteen years and Compeyson only seven, Magwitch vowed revenge. He found his chance when he learned from Pip that Compeyson had also escaped from the prison ship and was hiding in the marshes. It was that struggle that Pip had witnessed when the soldiers apprehended them. Magwitch was subsequently sentenced for life and transported; Compeyson, perceived as the victim of Magwitch's murderous intentions, received a light punishment. At the conclusion of Magwitch's story, Herbert writes Pip a note identifying Arthur as Miss Havisham's half-brother and Compeyson as Miss Havisham's fiancé.

Fearing that Compeyson will inform the authorities if he learns of Magwitch's return, Pip resolves to leave England with Magwitch as soon as possible, but he feels that he must first see both Estella and Miss Havisham. Arriving in his village, Pip encounters Bentley Drummle, who taunts Pip by stating that he plans to dine with Estella that evening.

At Satis House, Pip tells Miss Havisham and Estella that he is now aware of his benefactor's identity and suggests that Miss Havisham was unkind to allow him to keep his misconceptions about her for so long. "You made your own snares," she replies. Pip then asks Miss Havisham to undertake the subsidy of Herbert's position since he will no longer be able to do so. He then confesses his love to Estella. Unmoved, she repeats that she is incapable of love and then admits that she has made plans to marry Drummle in the near future. Pip is stunned to learn that Miss Havisham is against the match and that Estella is acting on her own because she is bored with her life. Looking at Miss Havisham, Pip notices that she wears an expression of pity and remorse.

Back in London, having been warned in a note from Wemmick not to return home, Pip visits the "Castle." There Wemmick tells Pip in a roundabout way that Magwitch's disappearance from Australia has caused "some little stir" and that Pip's chambers have been under surveillance by persons unknown. Wemmick also lets Pip know that Compeyson is in London and that Herbert, at Wemmick's urging, has moved Magwitch to a room in the apartment where Herbert's fiancée lives. He is to stay there until the time is right to slip him aboard a foreign packet-boat. Pip is told that he can visit Magwitch that night but must never visit Magwitch again.

Pip visits Magwitch and passes along Wemmick's news and advice, without mentioning Compeyson. To Pip, Magwitch now seems "softened." Herbert proposes that he and Pip use a rowboat to take Magwitch down the river. Herbert suggests that, to divert suspicion, they make a habit of rowing daily until the time is right for Pip to escape with Magwitch. Pip leaves feeling very heavy at heart, and for the next several weeks he lives in constant fear for Magwitch's safety.

Pip refuses to accept any more money from Magwitch and begins selling his jewelry to make ends meet. At the theater one evening, Pip's feeling of being watched is confirmed when he learns from Mr. Wopsle that Compeyson had been sitting directly behind him during the performance.

A week later, Mr. Jaggers invites Pip to dine with him and Wemmick. They tell Pip that Miss Havisham wants to see him "on a little matter of business." Suddenly, Pip becomes aware that Jaggers's house-keeper's features resemble Estella's, and he becomes certain that Molly is Estella's mother. After dinner, Pip learns from Wemmick that Molly has been in Jaggers's service ever since he cleared her of strangling a woman in a jealous rage. Rumors that she killed her own three-year-old girl in order to spite her husband surrounded the trial. Wemmick admits that he does not know what actually became of the child.

Literary Elements

The pivotal incident of the **plot** of *Great Expectations,* which helps define the novel as a ***Bildungsroman,*** occurs in Chapter 39. It marks the end of the second stage of Pip's development. Magwitch's revelation makes Pip realize how far he has fallen spiritually. At the end of this chapter, Pip is sitting by the fire through the night with the windows tightly shuttered and the doors barred, a **setting** reminiscent of Miss Havisham in her room at Satis House. In a flash of insight, Pip realizes for the first time that what he has is a sham, that his romantic expectations are illusions, and that his treatment of Joe and Biddy is his most ignominious behavior. As the hearth fire (the novel's recurring **symbol** for Joe) goes out, Pip realizes he cannot relight it, and he is left alone in absolute darkness. Spiritually too, he is in darkness and cannot see how he can ever undo the wrongs he has committed—that is, he does not know how to rekindle the fire in his soul. The storm that rages outside throughout this scene **symbolizes** the turmoil within him.

As the third stage begins, readers begin to see how Pip will redeem himself as he starts to shed the false pride he acquired in his pursuit of the genteel life. Pip's first act with his annuity is a selfless, generous one—to set Herbert up in business. As Pip's fears for Magwitch's safety grow and his cold attitude toward the affectionate old man softens, Pip begins to act selflessly.

Pip is not the only **character** undergoing radical change in these chapters. Miss Havisham, the victimizer, is revealed as the victim of her own obsession for revenge. Her retort to Pip, "You made your own snares," applies equally to herself. The ideal lady she created in Estella is incapable of loving men but also incapable of loving her. That sudden realization fills her with pity for the pain she has caused Pip and remorse for the inevitable pain that Estella will endure as Drummle's wife.

Theme

*   The **reality** of Pip's benefactor belies **appearance** as Magwitch reveals himself to Pip. Pip only reluctantly sees beneath Magwitch's **appearance** of a hardened criminal to the **reality** of his generosity, affection, and loyalty. When Pip does see the **reality** of Magwitch's character, he starts to act selflessly, and his redemption begins. Through Magwitch the complexity of the **present** is explained by the information he provides about the **past.** Unfortunately, decisions Miss Havisham has made because of her past also affect her current relationship with Estella.

*   Miss Havisham's **great expectations** of revenge through Estella backfire and prove self-destructive when Estella fails to love her and, despite her objections, plans to marry Drummle. It will be a marriage without **love** for Drummle; Estella is incapable of loving, for she has learned nothing but coldheartedness from Miss Havisham.

*   Pip uses his **great expectations** selflessly to help establish Herbert in business, commenting that his "expectations had done some good to somebody."

Chapters 49–59

Plot Synopsis

At Satis House, Miss Havisham agrees to give Pip the full amount needed to buy Herbert his partnership. She also offers to help Pip financially, but he declines her offer.

She expresses the hope that Pip will be able to forgive her someday, which he does immediately, replying that he harbors no bitterness toward her because he seeks forgiveness for *his* blind and thoughtless life. Repeatedly crying "What have I done!" Miss Havisham admits her fault in making Estella an instrument of her vengeance. Pip asks about Estella's childhood and learns that Mr. Jaggers brought her to Satis House when she was two or three years old. Miss Havisham had asked him to find an orphan girl for her to raise and save, as she says, "from misery like my own." Pip tries to console her, and then leaves.

He returns, however, to reassure himself that Miss Havisham is safe and calm. Looking into her room, Pip sees that her bridal dress has caught fire, engulfing her in flames. While smothering the fire with his cloak, Pip badly burns his hands and arm. A surgeon is called and reports that the burns Miss Havisham endured are not as life-threatening as the nervous shock. As Pip kisses her goodbye, she again asks him to forgive her.

Back in London, Pip learns from Herbert that Magwitch had a daughter, who was supposedly murdered by her mother. Pip realizes that Magwitch is Estella's father. Pip visits Jaggers, who confirms Pip's suspicions that Molly and Magwitch are Estella's parents. Jaggers then advises Pip that neither the parents nor Estella would benefit from this information.

With Miss Havisham's money, Pip completes the arrangements for Herbert to become a partner in the shipping firm—an act that greatly satisfies Pip.

One morning, Pip receives a note from Wemmick suggesting that Wednesday is the time for Magwitch to make his escape. Pip and Herbert make prepara-tions to row Magwitch downriver where he and Pip will intercept a steamer bound for Hamburg or Rotterdam. Herbert suggests that they enlist Startop to help in the rowing. Returning home alone that afternoon with the passports, Pip finds an anony-mous letter telling him to be at the sluice-house on the marshes if he wants information regarding his "Uncle Provis." Intrigued, Pip catches the first coach back to his village. Stopping at an inn to eat dinner, Pip learns that Pumblechook continues to accuse Pip of being ungrateful to him. Pip realizes with remorse that Joe and Biddy have never once complained of Pip's ingratitude toward them.

Entering the old sluice-house, Pip is restrained by Orlick, who ties him to a wall, reinjuring his burned arm. Blaming Pip for having him fired from Satis House and for coming between Biddy and him, Orlick intends to kill Pip and dispose of his body in the kiln. Pip thinks of the consequences his death would have: Magwitch and Herbert would think he had deserted them, and Joe and Biddy would never know how sorry he was and how much he meant to be true to them. Orlick tells Pip that he was indeed Mrs. Joe's attacker and that it was he that Pip stumbled over in the stairway of his flat in London. Orlick also knows that "Uncle Provis" is Magwitch because Orlick is a spy for Compeyson. Just as Orlick is poised to bludg-eon Pip to death, Herbert and Startop rush in, and Orlick escapes into the night. Herbert explains that he found the letter to Pip and decided to follow. Back in London, Pip spends the next day in a restless state of pain and anxiety. By Wednesday morning, however, Pip is well enough to begin the perilous escape.

The three row downriver with Magwitch aboard and spend the night at an isolated tavern. There they learn that a suspicious four-oared galley has been patrolling the riverbanks. When the group rows out to meet the approaching steamer the next day, they are intercepted by the galley, and an officer demands

Magwitch's surrender. Magwitch spots Compeyson aboard the galley; when he pulls back Compeyson's cloak to reveal his identity, Compeyson staggers back and the two enemies fall overboard. The rowboat capsizes in the steamer's path. After the three young men are hauled aboard the galley, Magwitch is spotted swimming in the steamer's wake. He is taken aboard and manacled, although he is seriously injured. There is no sign of Compeyson.

Accompanying Magwitch back to London, Pip realizes he no longer looks upon his benefactor with disdain. Instead, he sees a man more noble and more consistently loyal than he has been to Joe. Magwitch is content with his fate, saying that Pip can be a gentleman without him. Pip knows that Magwitch's fortune will be forfeited to the Crown, but he decides that Magwitch "need never know how his hopes of enriching me had perished."

Pip gets Jaggers to represent Magwitch, though there is little hope for acquittal. Meanwhile, Herbert announces his departure within the week for Cairo, where he will operate one of his firm's branch offices. He asks Pip to work for him as a clerk with the hope that Pip will someday become a partner. Pip promises to respond to Herbert's offer within a few months.

Pip visits Magwitch every day in the prison infirmary, where the convict lies in great pain and grows steadily weaker, but without complaining. After his speedy trial, Magwitch is sentenced to death. Within days, however, Magwitch lies on his deathbed. He thanks Pip for not having deserted him. As Magwitch's life slips away, Pip tells him that his daughter lives: "She is a lady and very beautiful. And I love her!" Magwitch's last act is to kiss Pip's hand.

Pip is now deeply in debt and seriously ill from his exhausting attendance upon Magwitch. When two men arrive to arrest him, he loses consciousness. He awakens to find Joe at his bedside. During Pip's convalescence, Joe informs Pip that Miss Havisham has died, leaving the bulk of her estate to Estella and four thousand pounds to Matthew Pocket. He also reports

that Orlick is in the county jail after robbing Pumblechook. Joe's tender care and conversation over the weeks make Pip feel like a child again, but as he grows stronger, Joe grows more distant and begins again to call him "sir." Resolved to express his feelings to Joe, Pip arises one morning to find Joe gone. A note explains that he no longer wants to intrude on Pip's life. With the note is a receipt showing that Joe had prevented Pip's arrest by paying Pip's debt himself. Humbled and repentant, Pip arranges to go to the forge and beg forgiveness.

At first, Pip cannot find Biddy or Joe. Finally he finds them celebrating their wedding day in the best parlor of Joe's house. Pip expresses thanks for all they have done for him and announces his plans to join Herbert abroad. Pip promises to repay them and asks their forgiveness, which they give gladly.

In London, Pip clears as much of his debt as he can before setting out to join Herbert in Cairo. Four months later, Pip is left in charge of the office while Herbert returns to England to marry Clara, and then bring her to Egypt. Years later, Clarriker reveals to Herbert Pip's secret involvement in buying him his partnership. Herbert is moved, and their friendship grows stronger.

After eleven years abroad, Pip returns to the forge to find that Joe and Biddy have a son named Pip, as well as a daughter. Saying that Pip should marry, Biddy asks if Pip still frets for Estella. He replies no, but adds that he has never forgotten her. He knows that Estella has suffered much in her marriage and was widowed two years earlier. At twilight, Pip walks to Satis House, of which only the garden wall remains. Among the ruins is a solitary figure—Estella. "I am greatly changed," she tells Pip. Her once proud eyes are sadder and softer, and she admits that years of suffering have taught her to appreciate that Pip indeed loved her. She asks that they continue to be "friends apart." Pip takes her hand, and in the evening mists he sees "no shadow of another parting from her."

Plot Synopsis and Literary Elements (cont.)

Literary Elements

Novel Structure: The novel's conclusion completes the *Bildungsroman* structure. The third stage of Pip's great expectations brings the protagonist to a point of maturity and insight, which would not have been possible without his experiences.

Themes

- In the final section of the novel, Pip loses his great expectations when the Crown seizes Magwitch's money and possessions. However, Pip's great expectations and accompanying false pride have hindered his moral progress. When he finally acts heroically, humbles himself, and shows increased love and loyalty toward Magwitch, Pip's inner nature changes and he becomes a "true gentleman." Pip may be able to fulfill his greatest expectation—his hope of marrying Estella. As Pip has, she has been changed by suffering. She is able to acknowledge Pip's true worth and the value of his love. In doing so, she makes herself worthy, finally, of Pip.

- Pip also learns that true **love** must be constant, forgiving, and unconditional—the kind of **love** he has always felt toward Estella, even toward Miss Havisham and Magwitch.

- Pip now fully understands that Joe's **appearance** as ignorant, awkward, and common is not **reality**: Joe possesses natural wisdom and tenderness and is truly uncommon in that he has the qualities of a real gentleman, such as honesty, compassion, loyalty, pride in work, and tolerance of others' shortcomings.

- **Ironically,** Estella, whom Pip had long considered free from the "stain" of crime, is the child of criminals. Though Pip keeps his knowledge of the **past** a secret from Estella and Molly, Pip tells Magwitch that his daughter is alive and Pip loves her. This serves as a final blessing to the dying criminal.

Symbolism: When Pip awakes from his fever to find Joe by his bedside, he feels like a child again. This **symbolic** rebirth represents the renewal in him of the spiritual values of Joe: simplicity, tenderness, honesty, loyalty, true pride, and selfless love—the essence of a gentleman. This idea of rebirth is extended by Joe and Biddy's naming their son Pip. Young Pip personifies Joe's love for the protagonist, his forgiveness of what Pip perceives as sins against Joe, and the promise of future expectations.

Satis House is a **symbolic** ruin at the novel's end. Among the ruins, Pip and Estella hold hands, suggesting a partnership that relies on human contact and genuine feeling, rather than on wealth and false hopes.

Reader's Log: Model

Reading actively

In your reader's log you record your ideas, questions, comments, interpretations, guesses, predictions, reflections, challenges—any responses you have to the books you are reading.

Keep your reader's log with you while you are reading. You can stop at any time to write. You may want to pause several times during your reading time to capture your thoughts while they are fresh in your mind, or you may want to read without interruption and write when you come to a stopping point such as the end of a chapter or the end of the book.

Each entry you make in your reader's log should include the date, the title of the book you are reading, and the pages you have read since your last entry (pages ____ to ____).

Example

Sept. 21

Fahrenheit 451

pages 3 to 68

This book reminds me a lot of another book we read in class last year, 1984 by George Orwell. They're both books about the future—1984 was written in the 1940s so it was the future then—a bad future where the government is very repressive and you can be arrested for what you think, say, or read. They're also both about a man and a woman who try to go against the system together. Fahrenheit 451 is supposed to be about book censorship, but I don't think it's just about that—I think it's also about people losing their brainpower by watching TV all the time and not thinking for themselves. 1984 did not have a very happy ending, and I have a feeling this book isn't going to either.

Exchanging ideas

Exchange reader's logs with a classmate and respond in writing to each other's most recent entries. (Your entries can be about the same book or different ones.) You might ask a question, make a comment, give your own opinion, recommend another book—in other words, discuss anything that's relevant to what you are reading.

Or: Ask your teacher, a family member, or a friend to read your most recent entries and write a reply to you in your reader's log.

Or: With your teacher's guidance, find an online pen pal in another town, state, or country and have a continuing book dialogue by e-mail.

Reader's Log: Starters

When I started reading this book, I thought . . .

I changed my mind about . . . because . . .

My favorite part of the book was . . .

My favorite character was . . . because . . .

I was surprised when . . .

I predict that . . .

I liked the way the writer . . .

I didn't like . . . because . . .

This book reminded me of . . .

I would (wouldn't) recommend this book to a friend because . . .

This book made me feel . . .

This book made me think . . .

This book made me realize . . .

While I was reading I pictured . . . (Draw or write your response.)

The most important thing about this book is . . .

If I were (name of character), I would (wouldn't) have . . .

What happened in this book was very realistic (unrealistic) because . . .

My least favorite character was . . . because . . .

I admire (name of character) for . . .

One thing I've noticed about the author's style is . . .

If I could be any character in this book, I would be . . . because . . .

I agree (disagree) with the writer about . . .

I think the title is a good (strange/misleading) choice because . . .

A better title for this book would be . . . because . . .

In my opinion, the most important word (sentence/paragraph) in this book is . . . because . . .

(Name of character) reminds me of myself because . . .

(Name of character) reminds me of somebody I know because . . .

If I could talk to (name of character), I would say . . .

When I finished this book, I still wondered . . .

This book was similar to (different from) other books I've read because it . . .

This book was similar to (different from) other books by this writer because it . . .

I think the main thing the writer was trying to say was . . .

This book was better (worse) than the movie version because . . .

(Event in book) reminded me of (something that happened to me) when . . .

Double-Entry Journal: Models

Responding to the text   Draw a line down the middle of a page in your reader's log. On the left side, copy a meaningful passage from the book you're reading—perhaps a bit of dialogue, a description, or a character's thought. (Be sure to note the number of the page you copied it from—you or somebody else may want to find it later.) On the right side, write your response to the quotation. Why did you choose it? Did it puzzle you? confuse you? strike a chord? What does it mean to you?

Example

Quotation	Response
"It is a truth universally acknowledged, that a single man in possession of a good fortune must be in want of a wife." (page 1)	This is the first sentence of the book. When I first read it I thought the writer was serious—it seemed like something people might have believed when it was written. Soon I realized she was making fun of that attitude. I saw the movie <u>Pride and Prejudice</u>, but it didn't have a lot of funny parts, so I didn't expect the book to be funny at all. It is though, but not in an obvious way.

Creating a dialogue journal   Draw a line down the middle of a page in your reader's log. On the left side, comment on the book you're reading—the plot so far, your opinion of the characters, or specifics about the style in which the book is written. On the right side of the page, your teacher or a classmate will provide a response to your comments. Together you create an ongoing dialogue about the novel as you are reading it.

Example

Your Comment	Response
The Bennet girls really seem incredibly silly. They seem to care only about getting married to someone rich or going to balls. That is all their parents discuss, too. The one who isn't like that, Mary, isn't realistic either, though. And why doesn't anyone work?!	I wasn't really bothered by their discussion of marriage and balls. I expected it because I saw the movie <u>Emma</u>, and it was like this, too. What I don't understand is why the parents call each other "Mr." and "Mrs."—everything is so formal. I don't think women of that class were supposed to work back then. And people never <u>really</u> work on TV shows or in the movies or in other books, do they?

Name _____ Date _____

Group Discussion Log

Group members

_____

_____

_____

_____

Book discussed

Title: _____

Author: _____

Pages _____ to _____

Three interesting things said by members of the group

_____

_____

_____

_____

_____

_____

What we did well today as a group

_____

_____

_____

What we could improve

_____

_____

_____

_____

Our next discussion will be on _____. We will discuss pages _____ to _____.

Glossary and Vocabulary

- **Vocabulary Words** are preceded by an asterisk (*) and appear in the Vocabulary Worksheets.
- Words are listed in their order of appearance.
- The definition and the part of speech are based on the way the word is used in the chapter. For other uses of the word, check a dictionary.

Chapters 1–9

pollards *n.:* trees with their branches cut back to promote dense new growth

wittles *n.:* vittles, dialect for *victuals,* food

battery *n.:* a military fortification equipped with guns

gibbet *n.:* a structure like a gallows, from which the corpses of criminals would be hung as a warning to others

connubial *adj.:* of marriage

*trenchant *adj.:* forceful; effective; incisive

*consternation *n.:* great fear or alarm that makes one feel helpless or bewildered

garret *adj.:* an attic

hulks *n.:* old, unseaworthy ships used as prisons

interlocutor *n.:* a person taking part in a conversation

imprecations *n.:* curses

penitentials *n.:* clothing that a penitent person might wear, *especially* black clothing

accoucheur *n.:* a male midwife

*appropriated *v.:* took for one's own use without permission

corn-chandler *n.:* a grain merchant

declamation *n.:* a dramatic, blustering, or pompous speech

*presentiment *n.:* a feeling that something unpleasant or evil will soon happen; a foreboding

intimated *v.:* hinted at; made known indirectly

hypothetical *adj.:* based on supposition

homily *n.:* a sermon

*commiserating *v.:* showing sorrow or pity for; sympathizing with

contumaciously *adv.:* in a stubbornly disobedient way

abhorrence *n.:* disgust and loathing

spasmodic *adj.:* characteristic of a spasm; sudden, violent, and temporary; frenzied

omnipotent *adj.:* all-powerful; having unlimited authority

*imperiously *adv.:* in an overbearing or arrogant manner

*vivaciously *adv.:* in a lively manner

apprehension *n.:* an anxious feeling of foreboding; dread

finger-post *n.:* a directional sign shaped like a pointing finger or hand

execrating *v.:* cursing

pilfering *n.:* stealing

exonerated *v.:* declared blameless and free of guilt

*venerated *v.:* deeply respected

perspicuity *n.:* clarity in statement or expression

*sagaciously *adv.:* in a keenly perceptive manner

farinaceous *adj.:* consisting of flour or meal

*discomfited *adj.:* made to feel uneasy

melancholy *adj.:* sad and gloomy

beggar my neighbor *n.:* a card game in which the object is to acquire all of your opponent's cards; *to beggar* means "to make poor" but also "to make seem inadequate"

caparisoned *adj.:* covered with trappings or ornaments

Chapters 10–19

nevvy *n.:* dialect for *nephew*

épergne *n.:* an ornamental stand with several dishes, used as a table centerpiece for holding fruit, flowers, etc.

sal volatile *n.:* an aromatic mixture used as smelling salts

*injudicious adj.: showing poor judgment

depreciatory adj.: meant to belittle

unremunerative adj.: unrewarding

indentures n.: contracts binding people to work for others for a specific period of time

*ostentatiously adv.: in a showy manner

*mollified adj.: made less severe, intense, or violent; calmed

Rantipole n.: a wild, reckless, quarrelsome person

*abject adj.: of the lowest degree; miserable; wretched

bound out of hand: made an apprentice immediately

*inscrutably adv.: mysteriously

excrescence n.: an abnormal or disfiguring outgrowth

*amiable adj.: good-natured; friendly

Cain: Adam and Eve's eldest son, who killed his brother Abel

Wandering Jew: a character in medieval folklore, condemned to wander the earth restlessly for refusing to convert to Christianity.

*morose adj.: ill-tempered; gloomy

George Barnwell: the title character of a popular play, in which an apprentice robs his employer and murders his uncle

Newgate: the principal prison of London from the thirteenth century until it was torn down in 1902. It was rebuilt after rioters burned it in 1780. Public executions were carried out in front of the gates of the structure, which was rebuilt from 1783 to 1867.

vexation n.: annoyance; distress

*disconcerted adj.: confused; disturbed

Timon of Athens: the title character of a play by Shakespeare; Timon is a bitter man who hates mankind

beadle n.: a messenger of a law court

Coriolanus: the title character of a play by Shakespeare; Coriolanus's arrogance causes him to be banished from Rome

*subterfuge n.: a stratagem used to hide one's true objective or to evade an unpleasant situation; deception

obtruded v.: forced upon (someone) unwillingly

*pervading adj.: spreading throughout

the rich man and the kingdom of Heaven: an allusion to Matthew 19:24: "It is easier for a camel to pass through the eye of a needle than for a rich man to enter the kingdom of heaven."

condescension n.: the act of dealing with others in a proud or haughty way

miscreant n.: an evil person or criminal

Chapters 20–35

hackney-coachman n.: the driver of a horse-drawn coach for hire

hammercloth n.: an ornamental, often fringed, cloth covering the driver's seat in a coach

equipage n.: a carriage used on formal occasions with horses, drivers, and liveried servants

portmanteau n.: a stiff leather suitcase that opens into two compartments

Covent Garden: a market area of London, famous for its many theaters and fashionable coffee-houses

magnanimous adj.: generous in overlooking an injury or insult

Handel: George Frideric Handel (1685–1759), German-born English composer

perseverance n.: the quality of putting forth a continued, patient effort; persistence

asseverates v.: asserts; states seriously or positively

the City: the business, financial, and judicial district of London

'Change: the Royal Exchange in London, where merchants meet to conduct business

collation n.: a light meal

Woolsack: the cushion on which the Lord Chancellor sits in the British House of Lords

mitre n.: an ornamental cap worn by a bishop

niggardly *adj.:* miserly

Brittania metal: a base alloy, resembling pewter, used in making everyday tableware

freehold *n.:* real estate that can be passed on through inheritance

*reticent *adj.:* habitually silent or uncommunicative; reserved

Macbeth: a famous tragedy by Shakespeare, noted for its scenes involving witches

obtuseness *n.:* the quality of being slow to understand, dull, or insensitive

*incongruity *n.:* the quality of lacking harmony or agreement; incompatibility; inappropriateness

Roscian *adj.:* pertaining to Roscius (circa 62 B.C.), a celebrated Roman comic actor

*lucid *adj.:* clear to the mind; readily understandable

Telemachus: the son of the legendary Greek hero Odysseus; during the father's twenty-year absence, the boy was left in the care of Mentor, a name that has come to mean "wise teacher and loyal adviser"

labyrinth *n.:* a complicated maze

*contrition *n.:* remorse for having done wrong; repentance

*culminated *v.:* reached the highest point; capped

Denmark: the country that is the setting for Shakespeare's tragedy *Hamlet*

contiguous *adj.:* near, next to, or adjacent; bordering upon

Ophelia: a character in Shakespeare's tragedy *Hamlet* who goes mad and drowns after Hamlet spurns her

malignity *n.:* an intense ill will and desire to hurt others

*facetious *adj.:* joking, especially in an ironic way or at an inappropriate time

ostler *n.:* a person who takes care of horses at an inn or stable

Lloyd's: originally a London coffeehouse, which due to its clientele developed into an association of merchants that specialize in insuring ships and publishing shipping information

Chapters 36–48

exemplary *adj.:* serving as a model or example; serving as a warning or deterrent

majority *n.:* the condition of having reached full legal age; twenty-one

ingenuity *n.:* the quality of being clever, original, or skillful

rubicund *adj.:* reddish; ruddy

impudence *n.:* the quality of being shamelessly bold or disrespectful

repudiate *v.:* to refuse to have anything to do with; to disown or cast off publicly

untenable *adj.:* that which cannot be held, defended, or maintained

the Temple: a complex of buildings which comprise the Inns of Court, where traditionally law students are trained

inhospitably *adv.:* in a manner that does not offer hospitality; forbiddingly

repugnance *n.:* extreme dislike or distaste

*aversion *n.:* an intense dislike

Botany Bay: the site of a former British penal colony near Sydney, Australia

physiognomy *n.:* facial features and expression, as supposedly indicative of a person's character

*impiously *adv.:* in a manner lacking reverence or respect

extricate *v.:* to set free; to release or disentangle

abyss *n.:* a profound depth; anything too deep for measurement

*insolent *adj.:* boldly disrespectful in speech or behavior; contemptuous; overbearing

incursion *n.:* a running in or coming in, *especially* when undesired; invasion

rhapsody *n.:* an extravagantly enthusiastic utterance

Great Expectations

*incredulous *adj.:* unable or unwilling to believe; showing doubt or disbelief

Hummums: a bathing establishment in Covent Garden, London, circa 1631; it later became a hotel

*despotic *adj.:* acting like an absolute ruler; tyrannical

Argus: in Greek mythology, a giant with a hundred eyes; thus, an alert watchman

packet-boat *n.:* a boat that travels a regular route carrying passengers, freight, and mail

Double Gloucester: a kind of cheese

antipodes *n.:* the opposite side of the earth

necromantic *adj.:* having to do with sorcery

Chapters 49–59

discursive *adj.:* in a skimming manner; rambling; wandering from one topic to another

*reiterated *v.:* said repeatedly

*magisterially *adv.:* in an authoritative, domineering, or pompous manner

*proffered *adj.:* offered

farden *n.:* dialect for *farthing,* a coin equal to one fourth of a penny

*detestation *n.:* intense hatred; loathing

plummet *n.:* a lead weight; something that weighs heavily

colliers *n.:* ships for carrying coal

*imperceptible *adj.:* so slight or gradual as not to be easily perceived

Jack: laborer; servant; attendant

Nore: a sandbank at the mouth of the Thames where it meets the sea

Hymen: the Greek god of marriage

bagatelle *n.:* a game somewhat like billiards, played with nine balls on a table having nine holes in a circular arrangement at one end

*indelible *adj.:* that which cannot be erased

coddleshell *n.:* mispronunciation of *codicil,* an addition to a will

*abstinence *n.:* the act of voluntarily doing without some or all food, drink, or other pleasures

*clemency *n.:* leniency or mercy shown toward an offender

*debilitating *adj.:* weakening or disabling

First Thoughts

1. When Pip steals from Joe and Mrs. Joe, he feels guilty even after he knows that he will not get caught. In your opinion, is Pip's feeling of guilt justified?

Shaping Interpretations

2. What are clues that Pip is narrating this story at a more mature phase of his life? What is the effect of this kind of narration?

3. The novel opens with Pip at the cemetery. From where he stands, he can see the marshes, the river, and beyond that, the sea. How is his view from this setting **symbolic** of great expectations?

4. When Estella complains of how common Pip is, Miss Havisham says, "Well? You can break his heart." Why would Miss Havisham say something like this?

5. Chapters 1–9 introduce three of the novel's important **settings:** the cemetery along the marshes, the house where Pip lives, and Satis House. In a sentence or two, describe each of these settings. In which setting does Pip seem the most secure? the least secure? Support your answers.

6. Considering the lonely and isolated settings in which the **characters** appear, explain how each of the following characters is lonely and isolated: Pip, Pip's convict, Miss Havisham, and Estella.

7. List two or three of Joe's character traits that Pip finds admirable. Explain whether or not you think Pip shares any of these traits.

8. At the end of Chapter 9, Pip is aware of "great changes" in himself. In what ways has Pip changed since Chapter 1? Cite examples to support your answers.

Connecting with the Text

9. Why do you think that Pip lies about what he saw at Satis House? What would you have done in his shoes?

Extending the Text

10. That was a memorable day to me, for it made great changes in me. But, it is the same with any life. Imagine one selected day struck out of it, and think how different its course would have been. Has a particular day in your life affected you this way? Explain.

READING CHECK

a. Whose tombstones is Pip examining when he encounters his convict?

b. Who interrupts the Christmas dinner at the Gargerys'?

c. Why is "Pip's convict" fighting with the second convict at the time of their capture?

d. List two examples of Estella's behavior toward Pip that he finds upsetting.

e. What are two things that Pip lies about seeing in Miss Havisham's house?

Writing Opportunity

Develop this response into a paragraph explaining the role that Miss Havisham and Estella have played in producing this change.

Reading Strategies: Chapters 1–9

Great Expectations

Writing Style

In *Great Expectations,* Dickens has a first-person narrator who is looking back over his life and telling his story. This allows him to make the story as suspenseful as he wishes, but it also allows him to make it very comical, by putting the sophisticated vocabulary of an adult into the mouth of a very small and confused child.

Using contextual clues, your vocabulary lists, and a dictionary, determine what each of these sentences means. Then, rephrase the following passages to read the way a child of seven might really say them.

1. To five little stone lozenges . . . which . . . were sacred to the memory of five little brothers of mine—who gave up trying to get a living, exceedingly early in that universal struggle—I am indebted for a belief I religiously entertained that they had all been born on their backs with their hands in their trousers-pockets, and had never taken them out in this state of existence. (Chapter 1)

....

....

2. In our already-mentioned freemasonry as fellow-sufferers, and in his good-natured companionship with me, it was our evening habit to compare the way we bit through our slices, by silently holding them up to each other's admiration now and then—which stimulated us to new exertions. (Chapter 2)

....

....

3. What if the young man who was with so much difficulty restrained from imbruing his hands in me, should yield to a constitutional impatience, or should mistake the time, and should think himself accredited to my heart and liver tonight, instead of tomorrow! (Chapter 2)

....

....

....

FOLLOW-UP: Dickens often creates humorous effects by using formal vocabulary to describe the everyday or ordinary. Write three such sentences of your own, using words from your vocabulary list or from a thesaurus.

Chapters 1–9, *Great Expectations*

IRON MEN

Pip was not happy forging ahead in Joe's profession. Working with iron requires working with the right tools, practiced know-how, and raw strength, as well as the ability to endure incredible heat. Because iron was known as the black metal and a smith is a maker, a person who made a career shaping and creating with iron was called a blacksmith. A smithy's fireproof forge is distinguished by a chimney perched atop a work building, with a brick or stone hearth inside. Blacksmiths were essential to village life in Dickens's time. Necessities such as cooking pots and farm tools were repaired, not discarded. Blacksmiths also made and fitted iron shoes for the horses needed for transportation and farm work.

INVESTIGATE
- *Research the current status of the blacksmith profession.*

PRISON CRUISE

After the American colonies gained their independence, England could no longer send its convicts to Virginia. Some 50,000 were sent before 1776. The retired man-of-war sailing ships that had transported prisoners across the Atlantic became floating prisons. These once graceful ships, that had proudly defended British interests around the globe, were moored along the Thames. There they sat, large, sad, ungainly vessels bobbing in a small space. Below the decks of these hulks, as they were now called, conditions were filthy. Tiny cells held men and women deemed the worst of those gone wrong. After Australia became England's new penal colony in 1787, many of the prisoners in hulks were transported there. England ended its floating prison system in 1858.

"Write about what you know"

Teachers often tell you to write about what you know. It seems clear that Dickens often did. In 1836, Dickens and his bride honeymooned in Chalk, a village not far from London where what is believed to be the model for Joe's forge still stands. It is now a private residence. Chalk village is in County Kent, the area in which Dickens spent his childhood. Other Kentish sights to look for in *Great Expectations* include the melancholy row of tombstones for Pip's family in Cooling, not far from Chalk. The Satis House belonging to Miss Havisham is based on a Tudor mansion, the Restoration House, in Rochester, a city south of Cooling.

Choices: Chapters 1–9

Building Your Portfolio

CREATIVE WRITING

Extra! Extra! Convict on the Marshes!

Write a front-page news story about the escaped convicts on the marshes. Provide an illustration or picture.

SOCIAL STUDIES

If I Could Keep Time in a Bottle

Imagine that Pip were going to create a time capsule of significant items from his childhood. With two or three other students, make a list of the items included, explaining why each was chosen. You may want to make an actual time capsule by putting models or drawings of the items listed into a box.

RETELLING

Ship Captain's Log

It is customary for a ship captain to maintain a journal of events that occur on his or her vessel. The captain or warden of the prison ship no doubt did so as well. Using facts from the book and your imagination, record the events surrounding the escape of the prisoners, the hunt for them in the marsh, and their return to the hulk.

MUSIC

Name That Tune

In the beginning of the novel, young Pip is looking at the graves of his family through the fog and beginning to cry. Suddenly he meets a gruff escaped convict. Dickens uses scary and suspenseful imagery in the opening scenes of the novel. What kind of music do you think he would have chosen for dramatic effect? Make some suggestions about the kind of music you would choose, and explain your reasoning.

ART

A Room with a View

Miss Havisham and her house are quite a sight. Using the description from the novel and additional research material if necessary for accuracy, draw either Miss Havisham or the room in which she sits day in and day out.

Consider This . . .

I do not recall that I felt any tenderness of conscience in reference to Mrs. Joe . . . But I loved Joe—perhaps for no better reason in those early days than because the dear fellow let me love him—

What do you suppose Dickens means by "tenderness of conscience"? How is Pip's love for Joe unconscious? How do you allow someone to love you?

Writing Follow-up: Compare and Contrast_____

Compare and contrast the behavior of a person who lets himself or herself be loved with that of a person who does not. Illustrate your points with references to characters in *Great Expectations* or other novels with which you are familiar, film characters, or, perhaps, personal experience.

Novel Notes

Create an activity based on **Novel Notes, Issue 1.** Here are two suggestions.

- Draw a picture of a hulk. Research the design of man-of-war sailing ships for accuracy.
- Locate pictures of other real locales in county Kent that Dickens includes in the novel.

Making Meanings: Chapters 10–19

First Thoughts

1. What is your reaction to Pip's behavior to Joe prior to his departure for London?

Shaping Interpretations

2. In *Great Expectations* the past seems to have a continual effect on the present. In Chapters 10 and 16, what two objects from Pip's past mysteriously reappear? What might the objects' reappearance **foreshadow**?

3. Identify three incidents that reveal Pip as a truthful storyteller. Then, identify an incident in which Pip seems to withhold information. Why do you suppose Pip does not always tell all that he knows?

4. Part of Dickens's style lies in his use of humor. Consider the following scenes:

- Mr. Wopsle's great-aunt's classroom (Chapter 10)
- Pip's fight with the "pale young gentleman" (Chapter 11)
- Joe's meeting with Miss Havisham (Chapter 13)

Identify the situation or language that makes these scenes humorous. What serious points is Dickens making despite the humor?

5. Identify two **external conflicts** between Pip and his environment. What kinds of **internal conflicts** result from these external conflicts?

6. In Chapter 18, Pip reflects: "[I]t is possible that I may have been, without quite knowing it, dissatisfied with myself." Explain Pip's dissatisfaction. Describe other characters who also seem dissatisfied.

7. I wondered . . . whether the flower-seeds and bulbs ever wanted of a fine day to break out of those jails, and bloom. One meaning of the word *pip* is seed. In what way has Pip been "jailed" like the "tied-up seeds"? By Chapter 19, in what ways has Pip begun to "break out" and "bloom"?

Connecting with the Text

8. Though Pip thinks of Joe as a friend and an equal, he is the closest thing to a father that Pip knows. Do you think that Joe is a good father figure to Pip? Explain.

Extending the Text

9. In Chapter 19, Pumblechook's attitude toward Pip changes. Describe the change. Do Pip's feelings toward Pumblechook change? What insight into human nature does Dickens's characterization provide?

READING CHECK

a. In what is Pip's shilling wrapped?

b. What does Estella allow Pip to do after he wins the fight?

c. With whom does Mrs. Joe quarrel the day before she is attacked?

d. What effect does the attack have on Mrs. Joe's temperament?

e. Who first tells Pip of his great expectations?

f. Where has Pip seen this person before?

Writing Opportunity

Compose a paragraph about Pip's **internal conflicts** involving guilt as seen in these chapters and those of the preceding chapter section.

Name _____ Date _____

Cause and Effect of Pip's Expectations

Pip literally awakens in Chapter 10 with a desire to make himself *uncommon;* thus begins one aspect of his expectations for the future.

Determine particular events and characters that inspire Pip's expectations, and explain what those expectations are in relation to that character or event. Then, consider the way in which Pip's relationships with others are affected by his new expectations. Provide a specific example from the text to support your observations.

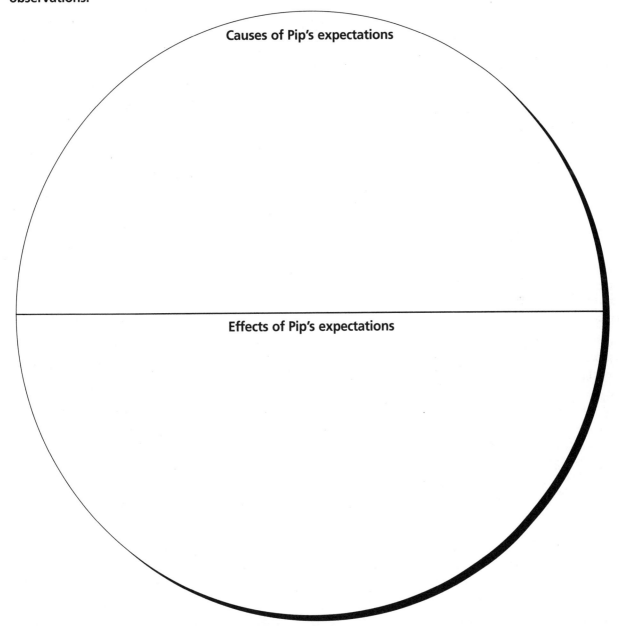

Causes of Pip's expectations

Effects of Pip's expectations

FOLLOW-UP: Predict possible negative and positive effects of Pip's good fortune.

Chapters 10–19, *Great Expectations*

FOR YOUR READER'S LOG

If you could apprentice with a master craftsman in any field, which field would you choose and why?

Schooling for the classes, not the masses

In Pip's time what you were formally taught, if anything, depended on your social class, gender, and, sometimes, where you lived. Upper- and middle-class boys and girls were taught at home until age 12 or 13. Boys then went to a public school such as Eton (public schools in England are synonymous with private schools in the United States) before university study. Girls stayed home and were taught skills such as drawing and dancing or went to a finishing school. There was no university study for girls until the late 1850s.

Village children of the lower classes could pay a fee to learn the basics in a "dames school" similar to Pip's. A church might offer elementary subjects in a Sunday school. In cities, charitable foundations set up schools, many trying also to feed and clothe the students. Institutions which charged no tuition were the "ragged" schools, so named because the students usually wore rags. Even with such charitable efforts, it is estimated that as many as one half of Pip's generation remained unschooled.

INVESTIGATE • *Research the university system in Victorian England.*

Learning a Trade

Before becoming a full-fledged doctor, a medical school graduate must first serve an internship, during which he or she is supervised by an experienced doctor. Apprenticeship, like today's internships, is learning by doing. When a master tradesman took on an apprentice, both agreed in a contract, known as an *indenture,* that the trainee, generally a young teenager, would learn while working exclusively for his teacher for a set time period, usually seven years. The apprentice then became a journeyman. Eventually the journeyman became a master.

A POUND OF CASH

Wouldn't it be great to have a couple of pounds of cash?

That all depends on what you mean by *pound.* As the United States uses dollars, the British use pounds. The nineteenth-century terms for coins in the novel can be equally confusing for the reader, unless you grew up in England. However, the following list may help you gauge the value of the coins used by Pip:

- pound: 20 shillings or 240 pence
- crown: 5 shillings
- half crown: 2 shillings and sixpence
- shilling: 12 pence
- sovereign: gold coin worth one pound

- guinea: 21 shillings or one pound one shilling (This coin was not minted after 1813, but the term for its value remained.)
- quid: slang for one pound
- bob: slang for one shilling

So, what is a pound worth in relation to a dollar? It can change daily—check in a newspaper or with your local bank.

Choices: Chapters 10–19

Building Your Portfolio

CREATIVE WRITING

Once Upon a Time . . .

The events in these chapters are a fairy tale come true for Pip. Write your own version of this portion of the novel in the style of a fairy tale for young children. Include all of the major characters and events, along with corresponding pictures that illustrate the action of the story. Your final product should be on unlined paper and bound so that it can be read like a children's book.

GROUP PRESENTATION

This novel has been adapted to fit the format of your TV . . .

With a group of three other students, prepare a television production of Chapter 10, 11, 13, 15, or 18 of the novel. As is necessary in a television show, you will need to provide pertinent background information so that viewers can grasp the story. You may also wish to add dialogue to make the story easier to understand. Film your scene, and show it to the class.

RETELLING

Job Descriptions

Evaluate how Wopsle's great-aunt, Joe, Orlick, and Pip (as Miss Havisham's walking companion) do their jobs. Then, create a job description or want ad for the positions which they fill. Many of these roles are described by Dickens with humor or sarcasm; try to maintain that same tone.

ART

Mural

Create a large mural on butcher paper of the story of Pip's life thus far. Choose objects to include that are representative of points in Pip's life. Include images that symbolize people who have influenced him. Use pictures and symbols, instead of words, to tell Pip's story. The mural should proceed chronologically. Use paint or markers, and post your completed mural in the classroom or school hallway.

Consider This . . .

"Biddy," I exclaimed, impatiently, "I am not at all happy as I am. I am disgusted with my calling and with my life. I have never taken to either, since I was bound. . . . I never shall or can be comfortable—or anything but miserable—there, Biddy!—unless I can lead a very different sort of life from the life I lead now."

What lifestyle does Pip not want to live? Have you ever felt the way Pip is feeling?

Writing Follow-up: Persuasion

Compose a two- to four-paragraph argument persuading Pip to look closely at *why* he is motivated to seek out a different life. You may want to advise the character to treasure the good things about his current life, even though seeking out a change may be a good thing to do.

Novel Notes

Create an activity based on **Novel Notes, Issue 2.** Here are two suggestions.

- Determine the worth of a pound in relation to the U.S. dollar today.
- Investigate what careers still have bonded apprenticeships.

First Thoughts

1. What does the word *gentleman* mean to you?

2. In your opinion, in what way does Pip become a less admirable character when he moves to London? Which admirable characteristics from his childhood remain?

Shaping Interpretations

3. In Chapter 20, Pip says he is fascinated by the **atmosphere** of Mr. Jaggers's offices. Identify this atmosphere, and list three details that contribute to it. Then, list four details of London and Barnard's Inn that help create a similar atmosphere.

4. Who other than Pip struggles with social position? Who is at ease with social position? What do you notice about Pip's relationships with those who are at ease?

5. In Chapter 29, Pip meets Estella again after several years. In what ways has she changed? stayed the same? In what ways has Pip's attitude toward her changed? stayed the same?

6. Once Pip has moved to London, his relationship with Joe and Biddy changes. What does this reveal about Pip's **character**?

7. What do you think is being **foreshadowed** by "the nameless shadow"?

8. Consider the **symbolism** or significance of character names: Estella, the Pockets, Havisham, and Drummle. Explain how their names reflect their role in the story or reveal some aspect of their personalities.

Extending the Text

9. Dickens often used his novels to draw his readers' attention to the appalling state of Victorian prisons. Considering Pip's experiences at Newgate Prison in Chapter 32, what prison reforms do you think Dickens believed were badly needed?

10. In Chapter 25, Wemmick says he keeps his professional life separate from his private life. Considering the atmosphere where Wemmick works and the atmosphere at his "castle," explain how Wemmick's personality changes to accommodate each of these settings. Through his portrait of Wemmick, what criticism do you suppose Dickens is making regarding the nature of work in a large city such as London?

Reading Check

a. Where does Pip reencounter the "pale young gentleman" of his youth?

b. What nickname does Pip acquire from Herbert Pocket?

c. Why did Herbert not particularly wish to become engaged to Estella?

d. For what profession is Pip to be educated?

e. Why doesn't the convict who gave Pip the one-pound notes realize Pip is on the same coach with him?

f. What realization does Pip have as he leaves the forge, following his sister's funeral, to return to London?

Writing Opportunity

Elaborate on the **symbolism** of Estella's name, providing examples of her behavior that reinforce this symbolism.

Reading Strategies: Chapters 20–35

Great Expectations

Tracing Coincidences

In the self-contained world of a novel, often a plot is driven by coincidences that other-wise would be improbable.

Trace the relationships between characters and the events in which they are involved that are connected by coincidences. Some information from other chapter sections may be necessary to illustrate the nature of the coincidence.

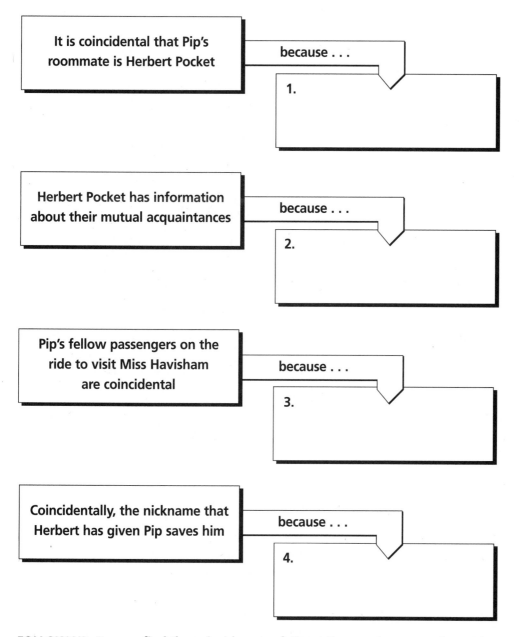

It is coincidental that Pip's roommate is Herbert Pocket

because . . .

1.

Herbert Pocket has information about their mutual acquaintances

because . . .

2.

Pip's fellow passengers on the ride to visit Miss Havisham are coincidental

because . . .

3.

Coincidentally, the nickname that Herbert has given Pip saves him

because . . .

4.

FOLLOW-UP: Do you find the coincidences of *Great Expectations* more fantastic than those in any other work of fiction you have read? Does this affect your response to the novel? Explain your opinion in a paragraph response.

Novel Notes

Chapters 20–35, *Great Expectations*

A Home is a Castle

Wemmick's house, with its medieval moat and turrets, indicates that he is a stylish, up-to-date Victorian. The Gothic revival in architecture was so popular that Gothic towers, spires, and ornate windows appeared on most public buildings built in that era, including the Houses of Parliament. The prevailing feeling among leading thinkers, such as the critic John Ruskin, was that Gothic architecture symbolized the high moral standards of Victorian society.

> **FOR YOUR READER'S LOG**
>
> What positive contributions might an aristocracy make to a society? What negative effect might an aristocracy have on a society?

What's in a name?

For Victorians, the answer to that question would depend on the title that comes before the name. The title indicates the level of peerage. Naturally, the monarchy is without peers; however, following the royal family are those aristocrats eligible to serve in Parliament's House of Lords. First among peers are dukes, followed by marquises, earls, viscounts, and barons. A duke is properly addressed as "Your Grace" or "Duke." Other peers are addressed as "Lord." "Sir" is the proper form of address for baronets and knights; although they are titled, they are not considered peerage, but commoners.

All titles in the aristocracy, except for that of knight, are hereditary and can be passed to the oldest male heir. The title of knight is a courtesy title awarded by the monarch. In the nineteenth century, knighthood was bestowed for achievement in battle, business, civil service, or the arts.

INVESTIGATE
• *Research which actors and rock musicians have received the title of "Sir" or "Dame" in the last two decades.*

Get me to the church on time

Weddings in Victorian England had none of today's pomp and ceremony.
• All that was required to marry was an announcement of intent in church (the crying of the banns) on three consecutive Sundays.
• A couple could buy a license, then marry in church or in the registrar's office.
• Until the 1880s, weddings were held between 8:00

A.M. and noon only.
• By law no weddings occurred with the church door shut (a centuries-old law to prevent a young woman or man from being kidnapped and forced into marriage).
• Only the bride received a ring.
Fashion note: While most brides wore white, any color was appropriate.

Different times, Different meanings

To Victorians, the term *making love* meant flirting or courting; this is what Herbert means as he tells Miss Havisham's story. A *lover* was a suitor.

Choices: Chapters 20–35

Great Expectations

Building Your Portfolio

Design a Wanted Poster

Choose a character in the novel about whom you have strong feelings. Brainstorm a list of his or her personality traits. Once you have a list of adjectives, choose a strong aspect of the character's personality for which he or she might be "Wanted." It does not have to be a negative character trait, just a noteworthy one. On your Wanted poster, include a drawing of the character, an alias, and, using colorful adjectives, a description. Describe where the character was last seen, and include something that the character is often heard to say so that he or she can be easily recognized. You may wish to include a reward.

CREATIVE WRITING

Poetry of Pip

Confessional poetry is a modern style of poetry in which the poet confesses his or her feelings, fears, disappointments, and hopes. Using what you know about Pip's first few days in the city of London and events that brought him there, write such a poem. You may wish to focus on one aspect of his life (for instance, learning about manners, becoming familiar with the big city, making friends with Herbert, or watching Jaggers interact with his clients), or you might choose to incorporate a number of ideas into your poem. The poem should be at least three stanzas and twelve lines in length.

READING STRATEGIES

Mapping Connections

With a partner, list all of the characters you have encountered in the novel. Create a map of how they are connected to each other. This could be a web, a tree (like a family tree), or another graphic. Use colors, and make an attractive display to hang in the classroom.

RETELLING / DRAWING CONCLUSIONS

To Whom It May Concern . . .

London struck Pip as dirty and grimy, but few places were more unpleasant than Newgate Prison. Re-read the Chapter 32 account of Pip and Wemmick's visit to the prison. Then, compose a letter to the prison warden from Pip's point of view. Retell Pip's experience with a slant toward reform of prison conditions. You may wish to research and include supplementary information about Newgate Prison during the mid-1800s.

Consider This . . .

"[N]o man who was not a true gentleman at heart, ever was, since the world began, a true gentleman in manner. He says, no varnish can hide the grain of the wood; and that the more varnish you put on, the more the grain will express itself."

What is meant by "gentleman in manner"? For what is wood grain used as a **metaphor**?

Writing Follow-up:
Compare and Contrast _____

Compare and contrast the behavior of Joe and that of Pumblechook. How might this quotation pertain to each of them?

Novel Notes

Create an activity based on **Novel Notes, Issue 3.** Here are two suggestions.

- Locate or research examples of Victorian-style architecture in your city or your state.
- Investigate which individuals have received peerages in the last thirty years.

First Thoughts

1. Do you find Pip's reaction to Magwitch appropriate?

Shaping Interpretations

2. Compare Estella's behavior toward Miss Havisham in Chapter 38 with Pip's behavior toward Magwitch in Chapter 39. How are their attitudes toward their benefactors similar and different?

3. Why do you suppose Miss Havisham objects to Estella's plans to marry? Explain how this objection signals a change in Miss Havisham's behavior.

4. In Chapter 44, Pip first sees Miss Havisham after learning she is not his anonymous benefactor, though he feels she has deceived him. She tells him "You made your own snares." On one level she is speaking to Pip, but on another, she is really speaking of herself. What has Miss Havisham recently realized?

Reading Check

a. What is the first thing that Pip does with his yearly allowance?

b. What upsetting news does Estella give Pip after he expresses his love to her?

c. How old is Pip when he learns the identity of his benefactor?

d. Who is his benefactor, and where has he been living?

e. How did his benefactor earn the money with which he supplied Pip?

f. In Chapter 48, what does Pip realize as he observes Molly?

g. What relationship did Miss Havisham have with Compeyson?

Writing Opportunity

Explain in a paragraph or two whether you believe that Miss Havisham is a **dynamic character,** one who changes as a result of the story's action.

5. **"But . . . I associate you only with the good, . . . for you must have done me far more good than harm."** Do you agree with Pip when he tells Estella that she has been the source of more good than harm? Explain your answer.

6. A **foil** is a character whose contrast to another character emphasizes the differences between them. How are the benefactors Magwitch and Havisham **foils** to each other?

7. What relationship do you think is being **foreshadowed** at the end of Chapter 48?

8. Why do you think Pip becomes increasingly concerned and fearful for Magwitch's safety? Explain how this increasing concern signals a change in Pip's personality.

Connecting with the Text

9. What reasons does Pip have for refusing to accept any more money after he learns his benefactor's true identity? Explain whether, in your opinion, these reasons are noble.

Extending the Text

10. The concept of a benefactor, a person who takes financial responsibility for another person, was more common in Dickens's time than it is now. Can you think of an example of a modern-day benefactor?

Name _____ Date _____

Reading Strategies: Chapters 36–48

Great Expectations

Retelling/Summarizing

Benefactor comes from the Latin *benefacere* meaning "to do a good act." In these chapters, however, Pip and Estella do not see their benefactors as having done them a good deed.

In the boxes and arrows provided, record the events that lead up to Magwitch's and Miss Havisham's becoming benefactors and the reactions of their beneficiaries.

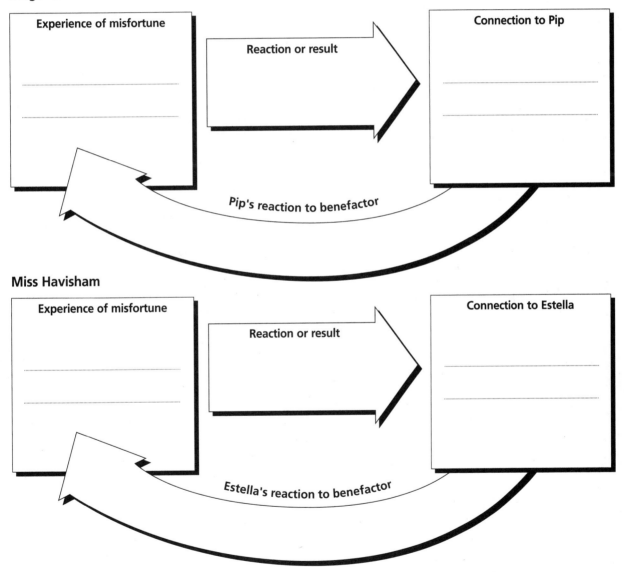

Magwitch

Experience of misfortune

Reaction or result

Connection to Pip

Pip's reaction to benefactor

Miss Havisham

Experience of misfortune

Reaction or result

Connection to Estella

Estella's reaction to benefactor

FOLLOW-UP: What is the ironic connection between Magwitch's tale of misfortune and Miss Havisham's?

Study Guide | **47**

Chapters 36–48, *Great Expectations*

The Rules of the Game

Old Maid is not just a card game, and the teenage girls of Britain in the 1800s knew that to reach the age of 25 unmarried was to risk being an object of ridicule and becoming one who had no role in middle- and upper-class society.

Young ladies understood the danger of disobeying the unwritten rules of courtship. Parties or dances, which were given for everyone, were an appropriate place for the unmarried to court. While a girl was expected to appear passive, she also could not spend too much time talking to an admirer. If he monopolized her time (trifled) without soon proposing, her value to potential suitors decreased. However, refusing a proposal would damage her reputation, because it was assumed that she had encouraged the suitor. Her reputation could also be damaged by her attending events alone or with an admirer. Therefore, families arrived and left together. Parents and friends kept a watchful eye on couples. If an admirer visited a young lady at home, a chaperone had to be present.

FOR YOUR READER'S LOG

Does understanding the courting practices of nineteenth-century England help you to understand Estella's decision to marry Drummle? Explain.

The Bachelor's Dilemma

After the mating dance began, a young man also had rules to follow. He could not appear too eager unless he could propose and marry soon. If he fell in love but could not afford to marry, he was expected to remain silent about his romantic feelings so the woman could marry while her chances were high. Long engagements were discouraged. A bachelor who proposed, or appeared to have proposed, then backed out, risked damage to his reputation and a lawsuit. Lawsuits for such breaches of promise were rare, however, because a woman's reputation was damaged more than a man's reputation. Consequently, most young women and their parents preferred not to expose such a social injury publicly. A respectable household (house, servants, many children) was expensive, and many Victorian men could not marry until their thirties. They typically chose a much younger woman.

Jumping Through Hoops

The fashion silhouette for women from the 1830s to 1860s was a tiny waist and increasingly full skirt. Layers of horsehair-stuffed petticoats were worn to create the "fluffed" look of the skirt. These were replaced by the crinoline or hoop, an undergarment containing up to 35 circular tubes. Sometimes dangerous on stairs and hard to sit in, the hoop was easier to wear because it was lighter. Women wore tightly laced whalebone corsets beneath their dresses to produce the desired 18-inch waist.

INVESTIGATE · *Research men's fashions of the day.*

Choices: Chapters 36–48

Great Expectations

Building Your Portfolio

CREATIVE WRITING

Journal Writing

Both Magwitch and Miss Havisham have long evening hours to themselves. Assume they spend some of that time recording their griefs or expectations for Pip and Estella. Imagine you are one of these characters, and create a series of four journal entries that he or she might write.

READING STRATEGIES

Extended Metaphor

The last paragraph of Chapter 38 is an extended metaphor—a comparison of two unlike things developed over several lines or through an entire literary work. Copy each sentence of the paragraph on a sheet of paper, leaving space between each sentence. Analyze the elements of "the Eastern story," and beneath each word or phrase write what it refers to in Pip's life. After you have deciphered this metaphor, write a one-sentence paraphrase in your own words.

GROUP PERFORMANCE

Speak the truth, you ingrate!

In a group of no more than four, dramatize Chapter 38. Select group members to play individual characters and possibly a narrator. Use Dickens's dialogue, dress appropriately for the parts, and use your classroom as a stage.

CRITICAL ANALYSIS

Gender Considerations

With a partner analyze the male and female characters in the novel. Create a two-column chart:

- List the principal male characters in one column.
- Describe each with two adjectives, and list two of their actions/decisions.

Make a similar chart for the principal female characters of the novel.

What do the men have in common? What do the women have in common? Who seems to be presented in a more favorable light? Present your conclusions orally or in a short two- to three-paragraph essay.

Consider This . . .

"What!" said Miss Havisham, flashing her eyes upon her, "are you tired of me?"

"Only a little tired of myself," replied Estella . . .

Look again at Chapter 38 for the root and the results of this discussion.

Writing Follow-up:
Cause and Effect _____

Explain in two to four paragraphs how being weary of oneself can be perceived as being weary of those around you. How does such a disposition affect relationships?

Novel Notes

Create an activity based on **Novel Notes, Issue 4.** Here are two suggestions.

- Research marriage customs among the working class during the Victorian era.
- Sketch a dress that would have been in fashion in Dicken's time.

First Thoughts

1. By the conclusion of the novel, do you think Pip has fulfilled any great expectations?

Shaping Interpretations

2. Pip has changed greatly by the end of the novel. Nevertheless, do you see any of his previous tendency to think only of himself in his returning to the village to ask Biddy to marry him?

3. The marriage of Biddy and Joe comes as a surprise to Pip. Find two passages in previous chapters which **foreshadow** this relationship.

4. Describe Pip's attitude toward Magwitch after the convict's capture. What does the fact that Pip will not inherit any of his benefactor's wealth reveal about the motivation of his attention to Magwitch?

5. What motivates Miss Havisham to offer financial help to Herbert and Pip in Chapter 49? Why do you think Pip refuses to accept any money for himself?

6. Pip's fever and recovery can be seen as a **symbolic** death and rebirth. Explain how Pip is reborn at the end of the novel. What parts of Pip have died?

7. **Irony** is the discrepancy between appearances and reality. Explain how Estella's parentage is ironic.

8. It could be said that Magwitch has not really been given a chance to become who he wanted to be. He has therefore dedicated his life to giving someone else his chance. About what other characters in the novel can you say this?

9. What does the relationship between Pip and Herbert reveal about the true nature of friendship? How does this relate to one of the major **themes** in the novel?

Challenging the Text

10. *Great Expectations* was originally written with a different ending. Dickens changed the book's conclusion because a friend persuaded him that the original ending would disappoint readers. How might you have ended the novel? Would you have opted for a happy ending? a sad one? Would you have Pip and Estella marry?

READING CHECK

a. How does Miss Havisham want Pip to show that he has forgiven her?

b. From what does Pip save Miss Havisham?

c. Where are Magwitch and Pip planning to go?

d. Why will Pip not inherit Magwitch's wealth?

e. For what city does Herbert leave?

f. When Pip first begins working for Herbert at Clarriker's, what is his position?

Writing Opportunity

Explain how this ending allows the novel to maintain the style of a **fairy tale.** Include in your explanation other elements of the story that are fairy tale-like.

Reading Strategies: Chapters 49–59

Great Expectations

Identifying Expectations

Pip is not the only character in the novel with expectations.

For each of the characters listed below, identify at least one expectation he or she may have had and how it was or was not fulfilled.

Character	Expectation	Fulfillment of Expectation
Pip		
Magwitch		
Miss Havisham		
Herbert		
Estella		
Biddy		
Orlick		

FOLLOW-UP: What role does Jaggers play in the expectations of many of these characters?

Chapters 49–59, *Great Expectations*

Time off for good behavior

Transportation to Australia was a ticket to freedom for prisoners who were industrious and well behaved. For many, Australia became the chance for a new start. Originally the penal colonies of Australia were forced labor camps. Gradually it became logical to hire out convicts to labor on farms or in towns, if the prisoners possessed special skills. Even those at the harsher colonies, such as Botany Bay, could work to reduce their sentences (7 to 14 years) through good behavior. Eventually, good conduct earned an absolute pardon, and the former prisoner could be granted Australian citizenship.

Felons transported to Australia were normally those sentenced to death, or violent, repeat offenders. The female convicts, about 15 percent of the prison population sent to Australia, were normally young repeat offenders convicted of drunkenness, not reporting to work, "misconduct," theft, or prostitution.

INVESTIGATE • *Research the types of criminals sent to Virginia.*

FOR YOUR READER'S LOG

How are events in the novel's conclusion clarified by this information about Newgate and debtors' prison?

Notorious Newgate

The carnival atmosphere surrounding executions added to Newgate Prison's notoriety. Conditions inside the prison were equivalent to medieval squalor even in the 1800s: Hardened criminals, women, and juveniles were jammed together in filth. Executions took place outside Newgate's high stone walls. Prior to the late 1830s, most condemned prisoners were hanged within two days of sentencing to maintain high public interest.

Huge crowds would gather, and many paid high prices to watch from the windows overlooking the execu-

tion site. When the hangings were moved inside, the public could still follow the action because of the parish bell that rang fifteen minutes before and after the execution. The description of the prison in *Great Expectations* is authentic, for Dickens was fascinated by the prison; he toured it several times and used it as a setting in three novels.

pack up, honey. we are moving to jail.

A debtors' prison was not designed for punishment, but for detainment. A debtor was arrested after a creditor filed suit, *not*

because of the debt. A bailiff made the arrest, and if the debtor could pay the bailiff immediately, then he or she could avoid prison.

If the needed funds were unavailable, the debtor's family could move in with "the prisoner." Visitors were also allowed.

Choices: Chapters 49–59

Building Your Portfolio

CREATIVE WRITING

Thanks a Lot

Pip and Magwitch each learn quite a bit from one another. Write two thank-you letters—one from Pip to Magwitch, and one from Magwitch to Pip. In each letter, have the writer express why he is grateful to the recipient.

PERFORMANCE

On Camera

Plan a televised interview with Uncle Pumblechook, who has been taking credit for being Pip's "first benefactor." Organize the questions so that the boastful Pumblechook will have to admit that he never really did anything for Pip as a child, except take him to Miss Havisham's house.

ART

The Capture and the Chase

Draw a six-panel (or longer) comic strip based on the events of Chapters 53 and 54. Remember that a comic strip need not be humorous; the tone of your strip should be appropriate to the tone of the book.

GROUP PROJECT

Chain of Events

[T]hink for a moment of the long chain of iron or gold, of thorns or flowers, that would never have bound you, but for the formation of the first link on one memorable day. Pip concludes Chapter 9 with this observation.

You and your group members are to construct a chain of events that links occurrences throughout the novel to the concluding events of Chapters 49–59. Use strips of construction paper wide enough for a written description of an event to form the links.

Links in the chain should be joined together because they are somehow connected. The connection between links may be written on the construction paper chain or orally explained to the class.

Consider This . . .

I sometimes derived an impression, from his manner or from a whispered word or two which escaped him, that he pondered over the question whether he might have been a better man under better circumstances.

What is your opinion of Magwitch's past? Do you feel that he has redeemed himself? Explain.

Writing Follow-up: Personal Reflection ▪

In a two- to four-paragraph response, reflect upon the role that circumstance plays in the type of person that one becomes. Do the characters of *Great Expectations* and their circumstances support your opinion? If so, how? If they do not, explain how they differ.

Novel Notes

Create an activity based on **Novel Notes, Issue 5.** Here are two suggestions.

- Research whether Newgate Prison or its buildings still exist in London.
- Investigate the Botany Bay penal colony.

Novel Review

▪▪

Great Expectations

MAJOR CHARACTERS

Use the chart below to keep track of the characters in this book. Each time you come across a new character, write the character's name and the number of the page on which the character first appears. Then, jot down a brief description. Add information about the characters as you read. Put a star next to the name of each main character.

NAME OF CHARACTER	DESCRIPTION

FOLLOW-UP: A *dynamic character* changes in some important way as a result of the story's action. In a paragraph, trace the transformation of one dynamic character from the time the character is introduced through the conclusion of the novel.

Novel Review *(cont.)*

Great Expectations

SETTING

Time ....

Most important place(s) ....

....

One effect of setting on plot, theme, or character ....

....

....

....

PLOT

List key events from the novel.

- ....
- ....
- ....

- ....
- ....
- ....

Use your list to identify the plot elements below. Add other events as necessary.

Major conflict / problem ....

....

Turning point / climax ....

....

Resolution / denouement ....

....

MAJOR THEMES

- ....
- ....
- ....

Name _____ Date _____

Literary Elements Worksheet 1

Atmosphere

Atmosphere is the mood or feeling in a literary work. Atmosphere is usually created through descriptive details and evocative language.

List three points in the course of the novel where atmosphere is significant. Then, describe the atmosphere in a few words. Finally, list the details and/or language that enable you to feel the atmosphere.

Point in novel	Point in novel	Point in novel

Atmosphere   Atmosphere   Atmosphere

Details / Language	Details / Language	Details / Language

FOLLOW-UP

- Choose two of the points, and explain how Pip was feeling at that time.
- What connection can you draw between the atmosphere and Pip's feelings at those points?

Literary Elements Worksheet 2

Great Expectations

Theme

One way to identify the themes of a novel is to consider what points about life the writer seems to be making. Some considerations when you are identifying theme are

- what kinds of decisions characters make, what their reasons are, and the consequences of their decisions
- what the conflicts (internal and external) are and how they are resolved
- what the main character learns in the course of the novel
- what significance there is in the novel's outcome

In the center oval, write down a theme in *Great Expectations*. Then, describe briefly one way that this theme is developed in each of the following sets of chapters.

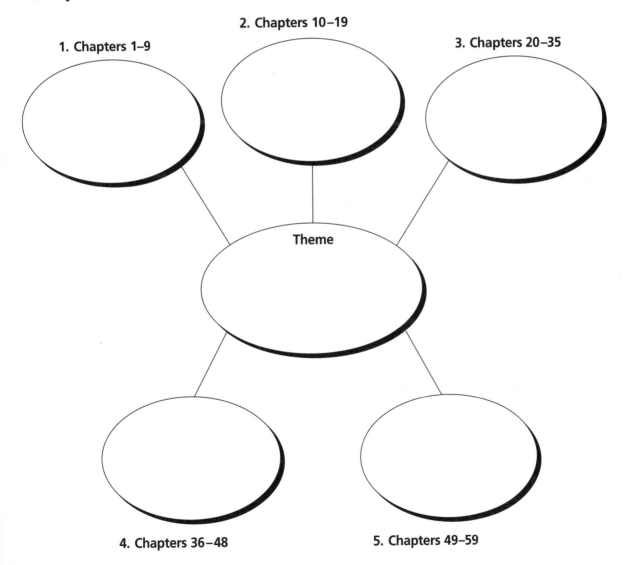

2. Chapters 10–19

1. Chapters 1–9

3. Chapters 20–35

Theme

4. Chapters 36–48

5. Chapters 49–59

FOLLOW-UP: Develop the information above into a three- to five-paragraph essay on the theme you have identified.

Literary Elements Worksheet 3

Great Expectations

Figurative Language

Dickens uses **similes,** comparisons between two seemingly unlike things using
the words *like* or *as,* to create images for the reader and frequently to provide humor.

**Read the following passages from *Great Expectations.* Then, on the lines below,
write how the use of the simile illustrates the meaning of each passage.**

1. On this particular evening the urgency of my case demanded a pint of this mixture, which was
   poured down my throat, for my greater comfort, while Mrs. Joe held my head under her arm, as a
   boot would be held in a boot-jack. (Chapter 2) _____

   _____

   _____

2. I struggled through the alphabet as if it had been a bramble-bush; getting considerably worried
   and scratched by each letter. (Chapter 7) _____

   _____

   _____

3. But Joe, taking it [his hat] up carefully with both hands, like a bird's-nest with eggs in it, wouldn't
   hear of parting with that piece of property. . . . (Chapter 27) _____

   _____

   _____

4. I went so far as to seize the Avenger by his blue collar and shake him off his feet—so that he was
   actually in the air, like a booted Cupid— . . . (Chapter 34) _____

   _____

   _____

5. [T]he two talked . . . as if they were of quite another race from the deceased, and were notorious-
   ly immortal. (Chapter 35) _____

   _____

   _____

**FOLLOW-UP: Using similes and language similar to that of Dickens, create humorous sentences of
your own describing the taking of medicine, an attempt at learning, the behavior of someone who is
nervous, an attempt to get someone's attention, and the behavior of guests at or after a funeral.**

Literary Elements Worksheet 4

Great Expectations

Bildungsroman

Great Expectations is a *Bildungsroman* or formation novel. Such a novel depicts the education or spiritual growth of the main character—usually a young man or woman—as he encounters various characters representing different attitudes toward life and undergoes moral crises.

Starting at the lower left and working your way up the left side and down the right, chart Pip's education in relation to the plot structure.

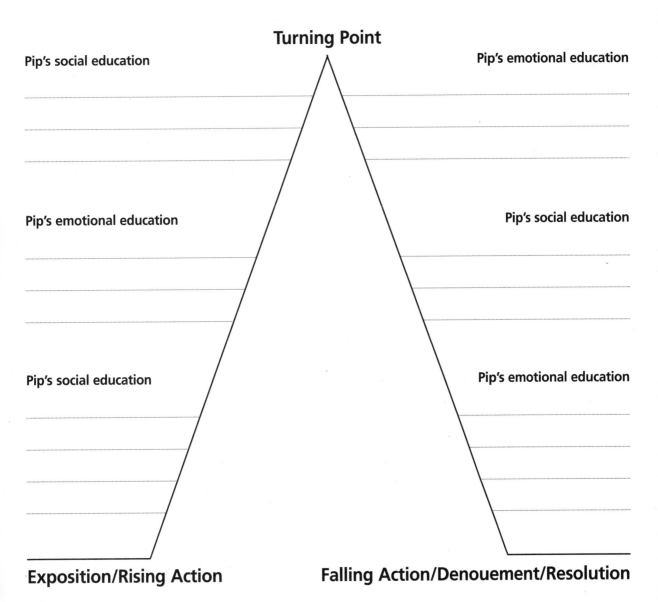

Turning Point

Pip's social education

Pip's emotional education

Pip's emotional education

Pip's social education

Pip's social education

Pip's emotional education

Exposition/Rising Action

Falling Action/Denouement/Resolution

FOLLOW-UP: Choose one of the lessons that you mentioned, and explain the event or characters that taught Pip this lesson and the effect it had upon him.

Literary Elements Worksheet 5

Great Expectations

Moral Fairy Tale

Some critics have described *Great Expectations* as a **moral fairy tale.** Indeed, there are many fanciful, fairy tale-like elements in the novel.

Assign characters, events, settings, and objects to the stereotypical fairy-tale element with which they correspond. (Some characters may have dual roles.) Explain.

Elements	Character, event, setting	Explanation
Knight		
Princess		
Fairy Godmother		
Wicked Witch		
Wise Man		
Monster/Ogre		
Castle		
Treasure		

FOLLOW-UP

- **What is the moral of this story?**
- **What elements of this story are grotesque or fantastic as in children's stories?**
- **How important is a happy ending to this fairy tale?**

Name _____ Date _____

A. Circle the letter of the word or phrase that most nearly defines the italicized word in each excerpt from *Great Expectations*.

1. Uncle Pumblechook . . . *imperiously* waved it all away with his hand, and asked for hot gin-and-water.
- **a.** angrily
- **b.** dangerously
- **c.** suddenly
- **d.** arrogantly

2. "Did you wish to see Miss Havisham?" "If Miss Havisham wished to see me," returned Mr. Pumblechook, *discomfited.*
- **a.** with authority
- **b.** without enthusiasm
- **c.** with an uneasy feeling
- **d.** in a calm manner

3. "He was a world of trouble to you, ma'am," said Mrs. Hubble, *commiserating* my sister.
- **a.** addressing
- **b.** sympathizing with
- **c.** explaining for
- **d.** accusing

4. "Well!" cried my sister, with a *mollified* glance at Mr. Pumblechook. . . .
- **a.** less severe
- **b.** slightly embarrassed
- **c.** mildly surprised
- **d.** bitterly sarcastic

5. We all began to think Mr. Wopsle full of *subterfuge.*
- **a.** cleverness
- **b.** nonsense
- **c.** stubbornness
- **d.** deception

6. The wonder and *consternation* with which Joe stopped on the threshold of his bite and stared at me, were too evident to escape my sister's observation.
- **a.** amusement
- **b.** alarm
- **c.** aggressiveness
- **d.** sympathy

7. Mrs. Hubble shook her head, and contemplating me with a mournful *presentiment* . . . asked, 'Why is it that the young are never grateful?'
- **a.** feeling of resentment
- **b.** laugh of pity
- **c.** sense of foreboding
- **d.** sigh of frustration

8. I *sagaciously* observed, if it didn't signify to him, to whom did it signify?
- **a.** sarcastically
- **b.** foolishly
- **c.** calmly
- **d.** perceptively

9. I particularly *venerated* Mr. Wopsle as Revenge, throwing his blood-stained sword in thunder down. . . .
- **a.** respected
- **b.** feared
- **c.** jeered
- **d.** cursed

10. For, it *inscrutably* appeared to stand to reason, in the minds of the whole company, that I was an excrescence on the entertainment.
- **a.** mysteriously
- **b.** strikingly
- **c.** obviously
- **d.** insanely

Vocabulary Worksheet 1 (cont.) Chapters 1–19

Great Expectations

11. That *abject* hypocrite, Pumblechook, . . . said, with a patronizing laugh, "It's more than that, Mum. Good again! Follow her up, Joseph!"

    a. absolute   **c.** miserable

    b. famous   **d.** harmful

12. I saw light wreaths from Joe's pipe floating there, . . . *pervading* the air we shared together.

    a. fouling   **c.** clouding

    b. spreading throughout   **d.** intruding on

13. He always slouched, locomotively, with his eyes on the ground. . . . This *morose* journeyman had no liking for me.

    a. lazy   **c.** timid

    b. dull   **d.** gloomy

14. My sister had a *trenchant* way of cutting our bread-and-butter for us, that never varied.

    a. funny   **c.** forceful

    b. casual   **d.** jagged

15. I am not quite clear whether these articles were carried penitentially or *ostentatiously;* but, I rather think they were displayed as articles of property—much as Cleopatra . . . might exhibit her wealth in a pageant. . . .

    a. in a showy manner   **c.** with help

    b. as if sacred   **d.** in a casual fashion

B. Read carefully the definition of each word. Then, write a sentence of your own using that word. If possible, include in your sentences clues to the meanings of the defined words.

16. appropriated: *verb,* took for one's own use without permission

_____

17. vivaciously: *adverb,* in a lively manner

_____

18. injudicious: *adjective,* showing poor judgment

_____

19. disconcerted: *adjective,* disturbed; confused

_____

20. amiable: *adjective,* having a pleasant and friendly disposition; good-natured

_____

Vocabulary Worksheet 2   Chapters 20–59

Great Expectations

A. Circle the letter of the word or phrase that most nearly defines the italicized word in each excerpt from *Great Expectations*.

1. "Yah!" cried Wemmick, suddenly hitting out at the turnkey in a *facetious* way, "you're dumb as one of your own keys. . . ."
- **a.** joking
- **b.** serious
- **c.** malicious
- **d.** angry

2. It was a sort of vault . . . with a *despotic* monster of a four-post bedstead in it. . . .
- **a.** filthy
- **b.** reckless
- **c.** spotted
- **d.** tyrannical

3. As he imparted this melancholy circumstance to Wemmick, Mr. Jaggers standing *magisterially* before the fire and taking no share in the proceedings, Mike's eye happened to twinkle with a tear.
- **a.** disinterestedly
- **b.** authoritatively
- **c.** happily
- **d.** threateningly

4. "You don't eat 'em," returned Mr. Pumblechook, . . . as if *abstinence* from watercresses were consistent with my downfall.
- **a.** overindulgence
- **b.** doing without
- **c.** a thorough dislike
- **d.** an upset stomach

5. I should have sat much as I did—repelled from him by an insurmountable *aversion*. . . .
- **a.** fear
- **b.** bewilderment
- **c.** dislike
- **d.** disappointment

6. But for the *indelible* picture that my remembrance now holds before me, I could scarcely believe . . .
- **a.** unerasable
- **b.** vivid
- **c.** unclear
- **d.** thoroughly horrible

7. "I forgit myself when I take such an interest in your breakfast, as to wish your frame, exhausted by the *debilitating* effects of prodigygality, to be stimilated by the 'olesome nourishment of your forefathers."
- **a.** harsh
- **b.** overexerting
- **c.** unlimited
- **d.** weakening

8. Estella looked at me merely with *incredulous* wonder. . . .
- **a.** terrified
- **b.** disbelieving
- **c.** terrifying
- **d.** unbelievable

9. The disgrace attendant on his immediately afterwards taking to crowing and pursuing me across the bridge . . . *culminated* the disgrace with which I left the town. . . .
- **a.** capped
- **b.** decreased
- **c.** offset
- **d.** began

Vocabulary Worksheet 2 (cont.)   Chapters 20–59

Great Expectations

10. This reminded me of the wonderful difference between the servile manner in which he had offered his hand in my new prosperity . . . and the ostentatious *clemency* with which he had just now exhibited the same fat five fingers.

    a. condescension   **c.** delicacy

    b. fairness   **d.** mercy

11. On the understanding, again and again *reiterated,* that come what would, I was to go to Mr. Jaggers. . .

    a. reworded   **c.** repeated

    b. exclaimed   **d.** hinted at

12. But as he sat gloating over me, I was supported by a scornful *detestation* of him that sealed my lips.

    a. hatred   **c.** pity

    b. fascination   **d.** analysis

13. [T]he misshapen creature he had *impiously* made, was not more wretched than I . . . .

    a. mischievously   **c.** regretfully

    b. foolishly   **d.** irreverently

14. By *imperceptible* degrees, as the tide ran out, we lost more and more of the nearer woods and hills. . . .

    a. unexplainable   **c.** almost unnoticeable

    b. darkening   **d.** strikingly distinct

15. [T]he *proffered* information might have some important bearing on the flight itself.

    a. valuable   **c.** offered

    b. secret   **d.** puzzling

B. Circle the letter of the pair of words that best expresses a relationship similar to that expressed in the original pair.

16. contrition : repentance ::

    a. glory : shame   **b.** bravery : valor   **c.** praise : condemnation

17. reticent : bold ::

    a. creative : artistic   **b.** shy : timid   **c.** knowledgeable : ignorant

18. thinker : lucid ::

    a. salesperson : traveling   **b.** miser : selfish   **c.** nurse : medicine

19. insolent : disrespect ::

    a. instability : solidity   **b.** rude : loud   **c.** compassionate : tenderness

20. incongruity : symmetry ::

    a. opposition: agreement   **b.** aroma : fragrance   **c.** water : humidity

Writing About the Novel

ALTERNATIVE ENDING

What Do YOU Think Happened?

The ending of the novel as it is printed in the version you are reading is how it originally appeared in the journal *All the Year Round* in the year 1860, but it's *not* how Charles Dickens originally wrote it. The ending as it stands is a "Hollywood" ending.

In your best imitation of Dickens's style, write the ending as you would have imagined it. Include a one-paragraph explanation to your audience of how your new ending stays true to Dickens's themes or how it alters the moral of the tale.

(Creative/Critical Writing)

ANALYZING CHARACTER

Stages of Growth

Great Expectations is divided into three stages, corresponding to the three stages of Pip's spiritual journey on the road to manhood. Write an essay in which you identify these three spiritual stages. Explain the changes in Pip or the events that mark his progression from one stage to the next.

(Critical Writing)

CREATIVE RESPONSE

Estella's Story

What brought Estella to the Satis House grounds the same day as Pip? What has she done in the eleven years that he has been establishing himself in trade? Develop an account of her life during those intervening years. Elaborate on the information provided regarding her marriage, but also create events in her life that are believable considering the time period and her personality.

You will need to decide the manner in which to tell her tale, including point of view and genre. You may wish to provide her with character traits that are not part of Dickens's account, but which are compatible with his portrait of her.

(Creative Writing)

LITERATURE REVIEW

Editor for a Day

Choose a theme from the book, and organize a portfolio of at least ten pieces of creative writing with the same theme. These can be poems, plays, or stories. Prepare a presentation for your class or an essay for your teacher that discusses the common thread in the writing.

(Critical Writing)

CREATIVE RESPONSE

But More About Me . . .

Choose one theme of the novel, and write a personal essay of four to six paragraphs about how the theme pertains to your life. You may wish to include pictures.

(Creative Writing)

COMPARE AND CONTRAST

Story Hour

At your local library, find at least two of the short stories that Charles Dickens wrote. Read the stories, keeping the major themes of *Great Expectations* in mind. In an essay, explain what relation the themes of the stories have to the themes of *Great Expectations*. You may wish to limit the subject of your essay to one story.

(Critical Writing)

Cross-Curricular Connections

MUSIC

Soundtrack

Choose a dramatic event in the novel, and write a musical accompaniment for it that you can perform for the class. The music should match the emotional tone of the scene you choose. Be prepared to bring a recording of your composition to class or to perform it for the class.

ART

Character Sketch

Young Pip wandering about in a cemetery. Miss Havisham still in her wedding dress but never a bride. Gentle, yet strong Joe at the forge. Mrs. Pocket with children tumbling all about her. Magwitch soaking wet on a galley, holding Pip's hand and headed back to prison. The images that Dickens creates are powerful. Re-create on paper one striking scene that captures one character's personality. Draw or paint this scene on paper or canvas at least 11 x 14 inches in size.

ARCHITECTURE

Structural Styles

Use sketches to compare the different architectural styles of some of the main buildings in the book: Satis House, Joe's house, Barnard's Inn, Newgate Prison, and Wemmick's house. Make a small architectural model of the building of your choice.

HOME ECONOMICS

Prince or Pauper?

Great Expectations addresses issues of social station and class. Choose one of the main characters in the novel, and sew a costume that would be in keeping with his or her profession or level of wealth and position. Research will be important for authenticity. You may wish to make a miniature outfit designed for a child or a doll.

FASHION/ART

Sketching for the Wedding

The last portion of the novel includes descriptions of several weddings. Research bridal clothing in England in the early 1800s, and sketch the dresses that you imagine the women might have worn.

SOCIAL STUDIES

Prison Reform?

Throughout the novel, Dickens takes the opportunity to show his disdain for the judicial system of his time. Research the laws that governed incarceration at the time, and write a report detailing penalty in relation to offense. Conclude your report with your opinions about the justice and logic of the nineteenth-century British prison system.

CAREERS

Iron Men

Using reference material from the library or the Internet, research the career of blacksmith. What might a blacksmith such as Joe have done? What tools would he have used? Are there still blacksmiths today? With the information you find in your research, create an illustrated booklet about the career of a blacksmith.

Multimedia and Internet Connections

NOTE: Check with your teacher about school policies on accessing Internet sites.

RECORDING: VIDEO

You Oughta Be in Pictures

With a cast and crew of fellow classmates, choose a stage of Pip's life to turn into a made-for-the-classroom movie. Actors should have lines memorized (or cue cards off-camera). You may wish to modernize your version of *Great Expectations*, but be sure that characters are appropriately attired to indicate social status and that your setting creates the atmosphere that Dickens was trying to evoke.

PRESENTATION: AUDIOVISUAL

Mixed Media Madness

Choose a section of the novel that particularly interests you. Write a ten-minute slide presentation based on this section of the story and its action, themes, and/or language. Record your script. Then, think of twenty (fairly simple) visual images that match the action. Using blank slides (which can be made from blank transparency sheets and slide mounts) and colored transparency markers, illustrate your story. Then, using the recording of your script, make a slide presentation to your class.

   If you have access to a camera that uses 35-millimeter film or to computer software that generates art, you may choose to create your slides from pictures you have taken or from computer graphics.

COMMERCIAL: AUDIOVISUAL

A Trailer

Write and record a commercial or a trailer for a film of *Great Expectations*. You will want to include visual representation of a particularly suspenseful, comic, or dramatic scene. Music will be necessary to create an appropriate tone.

SILENT FILM: VIDEO

Movies and Music

Choose a section of the novel that you particularly enjoy, and reduce it to actions. That is, make a "script" that does not involve any words, but is just a series of stage directions. Using students (or your family) as actors in costume, make a videotape of your film. Add music to match the action—just like a real silent movie!

WEB SITE DESIGN: INTERNET

pip.com?

Design a Web site for *Great Expectations*. You will want to include information about plot, theme, setting, and literary significance. Images should be incorporated to visually enhance your site. Include links to related sites such as Web pages about Dickens, prisons in Britain in the early nineteenth century, or other Dickens novels with similar themes.

BOOK ON TAPE: AUDIO

Get an Ear Full

Choose two chapters or a lengthy chapter that you find significant to the action of the novel, the development of Pip's character, or one of the themes of the novel, and record yourself reading this passage aloud. This is to be a dramatization of the chapter(s). Focus on vocabulary pronunciation, volume, intonation, and inflection. At the end of your reading, provide an oral explanation to the listener regarding the significance of this passage to the novel as a whole, the characters, or the theme.

Introducing the Connections

The **Connections** that follow this novel in the HRW LIBRARY edition create the opportunity for students to relate the novel's themes to other genres, times, and places and to their own lives. The following chart will facilitate your use of these additional works. Succeeding pages offer **Making Meanings** questions to stimulate student response.

Selection	Summary, Connection to Novel
A Dickens of an Ending Charles Dickens *original novel ending*	Not only Hollywood goes for happy endings. Dickens was convinced by a friend that his readers would have *great expectations* of Pip and Estella ending up together. He therefore never published this original conclusion to the novel.
Class, Tradition, and Money Sally Mitchell *social history*	Pip's struggle with social acceptance may seem exaggerated and unrealistic today. This account puts Pip's experience into the social context of the day and clarifies for modern readers the class distinctions that dominated nineteenth-century England.
The Rules of the Game Michael Brander *etiquette*	Emily Post *or* Miss Manners. Pip could have used their advice or the advice provided in this selection from two books of etiquette for Victorian gentlemen.
Interior Dorothy Parker *poem*	The inner world of the heartbroken woman described in this poem reminds the reader of the extent to which Miss Havisham goes in order to shield herself from the world and from her own heartache.
Casa Judith Ortiz Cofer *memoir*	This story-within-a-story tells how a woman deserted at the altar "allowed love to defeat her." Like Miss Havisham, María la Loca is a woman whose life has become defined by a promise which was never fulfilled.
Dick Whittington *legend*	Rags-to-riches stories have always had popular appeal. This legend originated centuries before Dickens's time and touches on the theme of orphans who rise above their station.
If— Rudyard Kipling *poem*	Pip aspires to be a gentleman. Not until the conclusion of the novel does he realize that being a gentleman is not about his station but his behavior. Kipling's poem is advice on the behavior and the perspective necessary to become a man or woman of quality.

Introducing the Connections *(cont.)*

Selection	Summary, Connection to Novel
The Prodigal Son Luke 15:11–32 *parable*	In so many ways, Pip is the prodigal son: Money takes him away from the only father he has ever known. As fast as good fortune came, it is gone, and Pip is saved by the unconditional love of Joe, who can be seen as his father figure.
You must know that I do not love Pablo Neruda *poem*	More than once, Estella tells Pip she cannot love him, yet only with him is she honest and only his feelings does she try to protect. Such confusion of love and duality of feeling is the subject of this poem.

Exploring the Connections

Making Meanings

Connecting with the Novel

Great Expectations is full of fairy-tale elements. Which conclusion best maintains that sense of the grotesque and fantastic? Explain.

1. After reading both endings, which do you prefer?

2. After reading the last paragraph of the original ending, what do you think was Pip's attitude toward Estella?

3. How is the **theme** of expectations handled in this original ending differently than in the revised ending?

4. Do you feel that Dickens compromised the novel by changing the ending of it? How does knowing about the change affect the way you feel about the book?

READING CHECK

a. Why did Dickens change the original ending?

b. How does Drummle die in the original ending?

c. In this conclusion, where do Pip and Estella last see each other?

Class, Tradition, and Money

Connecting with the Novel

Knowing what you now know about classes, name a character from each class in *Great Expectations*. Of what class was Pip originally a part? What was the highest level to which he could have risen? In which class did he end up?

1. **Even if a working man . . . could afford an expensive ticket, he would not dream of riding home in the first-class car.** Clearly, social status in Victorian England had less to do with money than with level of education, profession, or family name. How does this compare with social divisions today?

2. In Victorian England, a title was a symbol of status. What kinds of things (titles or possessions) signify status in our society?

3. Do you think that there is an aristocracy in democratic countries? If so, whom do you think falls into this class? Why?

4. Name at least three values that members of the middle class of Victorian England embraced. How did these values separate them from the aristocracy and the "lower" class?

READING CHECK

a. Which class did "clean" work? (Clean work is mental rather than physical.)

b. When would a working-class family in Victorian England have been poorest?

c. What was a landed gentleman called?

Exploring the Connections

Making Meanings

The Rules of the Game

Connecting with the Novel

"Censor" was the pseudonym under which O. B. Bunce published his etiquette book. Do you think that Herbert Pocket acted like a censor to Pip? Why or why not? Is there someone else who acts like a censor in the novel?

1. Do you believe that it is more mannerly to suggest that guests follow your code of etiquette, or to let them eat at your table without calling attention to their habits?

2. Are there certain behaviors or mannerisms that you sometimes wish people would follow at the table? If so, what are they?

3. Recognizing **irony** is sometimes recognizing the discrepancy between expectation and the realization of that expectation. What is ironic about the advice to "always seek the society of those above yourself"?

4. Why were the 1800s referred to as a "notably self-conscious and insecure century"?

READING CHECK

a. According to Arthur Freeling's book, what company should a would-be gentleman seek?

b. What was the proper thing to do with your napkin in 1890?

c. How should one eat his or her bread?

Interior

Connecting with the Novel

Compare and contrast the imagery of this poem with the description of Miss Havisham's room in Satis House.

1. What strikes you as most tragic about the woman described in the poem?

2. **Tone** is the attitude the writer takes toward the subject of a work. What seems to be the tone of the poem: objective, solemn, playful, ironic, sarcastic, reverent, or other? Explain.

3. What is the **rhyme scheme** of this poem? How is it effective in conveying the life of the woman described?

4. How does the **imagery,** the language used to evoke a picture or sensation, in the last three lines differ from the imagery in the rest of the poem?

READING CHECK

a. To what does the poem title "Interior" refer?

b. Who are the two "characters" in this poem?

Casa

Connecting with the Novel

What role do both Miss Havisham and María la Loca play in their respective communities?

1. From the narrator's description of her two homes, which would you prefer? Why?

2. From the context, what do you think "la Loca" means?

3. Why do Mamá and her daughters sit and retell the same stories, changing the details but never the moral?

4. How does Mamá's braiding of the narrator's hair throughout her storytelling act as a **symbol** for the café con leche hour?

READING CHECK

a. In what two places does the narrator live?

b. Who gathers in Mamá's living room?

Making Meanings

Dick Whittington

Connecting with the Novel

In what way is Dick Whittington like Pip? In what way does he differ from Pip?

1. Why do you suppose "rags-to-riches" stories have always been popular?

2. What does this story have in common with fairy tales you have heard or read?

3. Describe Dick Whittington's character. Support your opinion with examples of his actions.

4. Identify an instance of **foreshadowing** in the legend.

5. A legend, like a fairy tale, often has a moral. What is the moral of this legend?

> **READING CHECK**
>
> **a.** What had Dick Whittington heard about the streets of London?
>
> **b.** How much did Dick Whittington pay for his cat?
>
> **c.** What made the cat so valuable?

If—

Connecting with the Novel

Provide examples of Pip falling short of the behavior described in this poem and examples of Pip fulfilling Kipling's ideal.

1. What do you think is the best advice the speaker gives?

2. Why do you suppose Kipling capitalizes *Triumph, Disaster,* and *Will*?

3. What would be the value in treating "Triumph and Disaster . . . just the same"?

4. *If* indicates a condition, a supposition, or a qualification. Consider the title of the poem and the use of the word *if* in the stanzas. How does the speaker structure his advice around conditions, suppositions, or qualifications?

5. Explain the significance of the last line: "And—which is more—you'll be a Man, my son!"

> **READING CHECK**
>
> **a.** According to the poem, "when all men doubt you" what should you do?
>
> **b.** According to the speaker, what would be admirable behavior after you have lost all your winnings?
>
> **c.** What is the object of the speaker's advice?

Making Meanings

The Prodigal Son

Connecting with the Novel

How do the thoughts and behavior of Pip and Joe mirror those of the characters in this parable?

1. What actions of the son do you find realistic and understandable? Explain.

2. What do neither the younger son nor the elder realize about their father?

3. What is one **theme,** insight into life, found within this passage and also present in *Great Expectations?*

4. Parables, like fairy tales, are a **genre** (type) of writing. Based on your experience with this parable and fairy tales, what similarity do you see between these genres?

READING CHECK

a. What made the prodigal son realize he should return to his father?

b. How was the son going to ask to be treated?

You must know that I do not love

Connecting with the Novel

Does this poem remind you of any relationships in *Great Expectations?* Why?

1. Why do you think that confused or unrequited love is such a common theme in literature?

2. How does "fire has its cold half" summarize the speaker's divided feelings?

3. What words are the "keys" that the speaker holds? How is the speaker influenced by what those words may unlock?

4. The speaker repeatedly expresses the thought that he or she is divided or of two minds. What in the final stanza contradicts that image?

READING CHECK

Why does the speaker claim not to love?

TEST   PART I: OBJECTIVE QUESTIONS

A. Directions: Match each character with the correct description. Write the letter of the best choice in the corresponding numbered blank. *(15 points)*

_____ **1.** Trabb's boy

_____ **2.** Miss Havisham

_____ **3.** Joe Gargery

_____ **4.** Mrs. Joe

_____ **5.** Estella

_____ **6.** Molly

_____ **7.** Uncle Provis

_____ **8.** Mr. Jaggers

_____ **9.** Mr. Pumblechook

_____ **10.** Biddy

_____ **11.** Orlick

_____ **12.** Herbert Pocket

_____ **13.** Wemmick

_____ **14.** Compeyson

_____ **15.** Matthew Pocket

a. teaches Pip to read

b. pays Pip's debts

c. lives in a replica of a castle

d. marries Bentley Drummle

e. acts as Pip's guardian in London

f. helps Pip, financially, to buy Herbert's partnership

g. proposed marriage to Miss Havisham

h. challenges Pip to a boxing match

i. tutors Pip in London

j. tries to kill Pip

k. claims to have helped to establish Pip as a gentleman

l. gives up her daughter for adoption

m. alias for Magwitch

n. was wounded by Orlick

o. mocks Pip

B. Directions: In the spaces provided, mark each true statement *T* and each false statement *F*. (20 points)

_____ **16.** All the clocks at Miss Havisham's are stopped at ten o'clock.

_____ **17.** In London, Pip lives at Barnard's Inn and at the Pockets' house.

_____ **18.** The Aged is Pip's servant.

_____ **19.** The money Pip receives from his secret benefactor was gained illegally through a life of crime.

_____ **20.** When Pip comes into his good fortune, he soon acquires extravagant habits.

_____ **21.** Estella is devastated when Pip tells her who her real parents are.

_____ **22.** After Miss Havisham's death, Estella moves to Satis House and has it restored to its former splendor.

_____ **23.** Miss Havisham leaves Pip a handsome amount of money in her will.

_____ **24.** Wemmick, Estella, Herbert, and Joe marry in the course of the novel.

_____ **25.** After Magwitch is apprehended while trying to flee England, he is tried, sentenced to death, and publicly executed before the gates of Newgate Prison.

Name _____ Date _____

TEST ▮▮▮ PART II: SHORT-ANSWER QUESTIONS

Answer each question, using the lines provided. (40 points)

26. How does Pip first make the acquaintance of Magwitch, and why is the criminal so grateful to Pip?

_____

_____

_____

27. What is Pip's relationship to Joe and Mrs. Joe? Explain how Pip gets along with each of these characters at the beginning of the novel.

_____

_____

_____

28. When does Pip first begin to worry about his status?

_____

_____

_____

29. Why does Miss Havisham wear a wedding dress all the time?

_____

_____

_____

30. Explain the two personalities of Wemmick.

_____

_____

_____

TEST PART II: SHORT-ANSWER QUESTIONS

31. What are two conditions placed on Pip by his benefactor in order for him to receive his fortune?

....

....

....

32. Why does Wemmick leave Pip a note asking him not to return to his quarters in London after he has been away at Satis House?

....

....

....

33. At one point in the novel, Estella and Miss Havisham quarrel. Explain why.

....

....

....

34. Who are Estella's parents, and how did she come to be raised by Miss Havisham?

....

....

....

35. Why, at one point in the novel, is Pip on the verge of being arrested? Who keeps Pip out of prison?

....

....

....

TEST   PART III: ESSAY QUESTIONS

Choose two of the following topics. Use your own paper to write two or three paragraphs about each topic you choose. *(25 points)*

a. *Great Expectations* has been described as a **Bildungsroman**—a novel tracing the education and spiritual growth of a young protagonist. Choose one lesson that Pip learns, and trace his education on that issue throughout the novel.

b. *Great Expectations* contains many details that **foreshadow,** or predict, later events. Identify at least one detail that foreshadows each of the following incidents:
  • Magwitch's revelation that he is Pip's benefactor
  • Orlick's attempt to murder Pip
  • Pip's realization that Molly is Estella's biological mother
  • the marriage of Joe and Biddy

c. Some critics argue that because Dickens wants his reader to view the story from a child's perspective, he purposely draws on the conventions of **fairy tales** in creating his plot, characters, and settings. What evidence is there in the novel to support this view? Do you think the connection to fairy tales adds to or detracts from the impact of the novel? Write an essay in which you answer these two questions. Consider the following elements in your evaluation:

  • coincidences that would be unbelievable in real life
  • characters that resemble witches, evil step-mothers, larger-than-life villains, fairy god-mothers, ogres, beautiful princesses, and frogs disguised as princes
  • fantastic or make-believe settings

d. Dickens used his novels to bring attention to social injustices that he saw in English society. Explain how Dickens portrays Abel Magwitch as a victim of English law and social prejudice.

e. For much of the novel, Miss Havisham is a symbol of life in suspension, of stagnation and arrested growth. Eventually, however, she does change. Explain why Miss Havisham can be called a **dynamic character,** that is, one who changes during the course of the novel.

f. Discuss how one of the Connections from the back of the novel (HRW LIBRARY edition) is related to a theme, issue, or character in *Great Expectations.*

Use this space to make notes.

Answer Key

Answer Key

Chapters 1–9

■ Making Meanings

READING CHECK

a. Pip is examining the gravestones of his mother and father and his five brothers.

b. Soldiers searching for escaped prisoners come to the house.

c. Pip's convict wants to prevent the other convict from escaping and to return him to the prison ship.

d. Responses will vary. Students should list examples of Estella's behavior that upset Pip, such as Estella calling Pip "boy," her "scornful" tone, her conception of him as "a common labouring-boy," and her delight in reducing him to tears.

e. Pip tells his sister, Mr. Pumblechook, and Joe that Miss Havisham was sitting in a black velvet coach, that they had cake and wine on gold plates, that there were four large dogs eating veal cutlets out of a silver basket, and that he, Estella, and Miss Havisham had played with flags. He also talks of swords and pistols.

---

1. Responses will vary, but students are likely to believe that Pip was not at fault because he was threatened, because what he took had little value, and because they feel sorry for him.

2. Clues that the novel is written by a mature author include the sophisticated vocabulary and the insight into the effects of events, such as the encounter at Miss Havisham's. Having an adult tell the story of a child can have a comic effect and can allow the events to be described in proportion to their later significance.

3. Responses will vary. Marshes are stagnant, as Pip's life could become if he does not aspire to things beyond what the village can offer. The movement of the river symbolizes Pip's progression from the forge to Miss Havisham's, where he learns to yearn for "greater" things. Like the river, he will eventually reach a larger place—London—as the river flows to the sea.

4. Miss Havisham has had her heart broken and is full of vengeful feelings.

5. Responses will vary. Students should describe the three settings in a manner similar to the following:

- The marshes include the cemetery alongside a church "down by the river, within . . . twenty miles of the sea." It is a bleak place, shrouded in mists, with a gibbet nearby, a deserted battery, and the prison ships anchored in the distance.

- The wooden house is typical of those in the countryside, consisting of a kitchen and parlor, and upstairs bedrooms. It is meticulously maintained by Mrs. Joe. Joe's forge adjoins the house.

- Satis House is a large brick mansion in the wealthy section of the village. It is a dismal place, with both barred and walled-up windows. It has a courtyard, an overgrown garden, and a deserted brewery attached to it. Inside, the passageways are dark and mysterious; the rooms are richly furnished but in a state of decay.

Students' responses will vary regarding Pip's feeling of security and insecurity in these settings. Students should realize, however, that at this stage of the novel Pip is least secure about Satis House: His treatment at the hands of its inhabitants entirely undermines his self-confidence. Students may argue that Pip feels most secure among the mists of the marshes, despite his terrifying encounter with the convict: He returns there twice, first alone with the food and file, and then on the shoulders of Joe during the hunt. At home, Pip must endure the cruelty of his sister's rampages, and though Joe's presence is a comfort to Pip, he lives in constant fear of his sister's physical and verbal abuse.

6. Responses will vary. Most of the following points should be included in the students' responses: It is in the isolated, lonely marshes that Pip first becomes aware that he is an orphan. At home he is treated as an outcast by everyone but Joe.

At Satis House, Pip becomes aware of his low, working-class status and is treated as an outsider by Estella. Pip's convict is, by law, an outcast from society. As an escapee, he is truly alone in the world. Miss Havisham lives in her own kind of prison ship behind the barred and walled-up windows of Satis House. She is physically isolated from society and from the natural world. Estella shares the isolation of Miss Havisham's house. She plays alone atop the casks in the brewery and spurns Pip's company.

7. Responses will vary. Students should note at least two of the following character traits of Joe that Pip appreciates: good nature, even temper, tenderness, generosity, and simplicity. Students may say that, as a child, Pip shares all of these traits with the man he admires.

8. Responses will vary. By the end of Chapter 9, Pip has grown in awareness, both of himself and of the world. His childhood innocence is gradually replaced by a sense of his deficiencies—and Joe's. Students will likely attribute this sense of inadequacy to the influence of Miss Havisham and Estella. Students might contrast Pip's letter to Joe (Chapter 7) with his awareness that he has "learnt next to nothing" (Chapter 9), or cite similar contrasts.

9. Responses will vary, but students will most likely see that Pip lies because he does not know what to make of Miss Havisham and Satis House, because the experience scared him and made him feel inferior, and because he does not want to betray Miss Havisham by truthfully describing her. They also may point out that he is generally frustrated by and angry about the way his sister and Mr. Pumblechook treat him; he feels he must entertain them or he will be punished.

10. Responses will vary. Students should not be expected to share personal details with the class.

■ Reading Strategies

Writing Style

Responses will vary. Sample responses follow.

1. The shapes of the graves of my five brothers who died when they were babies made me think that they had been born with their hands in their pockets and had never taken them out.

2. Joe and I were friends because we had a lot in common (being mistreated by Mrs. Joe), and part of our bond was to compare the bite marks in our bread, which inspired us to take even bigger bites.

3. What if the young man that the convict was talking about couldn't wait any longer to plunge his hands into me (to get my internal organs), or got the time wrong and thought that he was allowed to eat my heart and liver tonight instead of tomorrow!

Follow-up: Accept responses that show an effort to communicate with an expanded vocabulary.

Chapters 10–19

■ Making Meanings

> **READING CHECK**
> a. Pip's shilling is wrapped in two one-pound notes.
> b. Estella allows Pip to kiss her cheek.
> c. Mrs. Joe quarrels with Orlick the day before she is attacked.
> d. Mrs. Joe's temperament is greatly improved after the attack.
> e. Miss Havisham's lawyer, Mr. Jaggers, first tells Pip of his great expectations.
> f. Pip recognizes him from Miss Havisham's house.

1. Responses will vary. Many students will think Pip is behaving ungratefully and may feel he should return and make amends. Others may understand the dissatisfaction with life at the forge that manifests itself in his rejection of Joe.

2. In Chapter 10, Pip sees a strange man stir his drink with the file that Pip stole from Joe. In Chapter 16, it is revealed that Mrs. Joe was struck with the filed-off leg iron that Pip's convict wore. The objects suggest that the secret relationship between Pip and "his convict" will continue and that the convict himself will reappear later in the novel.

3. Responses will vary. Students should identify at least three events that reveal his honesty, such as his encounter with the convict, the convict's capture, Joe's meeting with Miss Havisham, and his argument with Biddy. Students should then cite some information that Pip the adult narrator withholds from the reader, such as the identities of the two convicts and of Pip's benefactor. Students should explain that he withholds such information so that the readers will have the same knowledge as Pip the child does at each stage of his development, and so that the reader will be kept in suspense.

4. Responses will vary. Students should explain the humor and the serious point of the scenes in a manner similar to the following:

   • Mr. Wopsle's great-aunt's classroom is lampooned as the epitome of educational chaos. Details describing the teacher's falling into a "state of coma" and the children's emerging "into the air with shrieks of intellectual victory" add to the humor of the scene. Underlying the humor, however, is Dickens's criticism of England's inadequate educational system for lower-class children.

   • The dialogue of Miss Havisham's relatives proves that they are, as Pip observes, "toadies and humbugs." Miss Havisham, for all her eccentricity, sees them clearly for what they are and can barely keep her sarcasm in check as she sweeps past them, propelled in her wheelchair by Pip. The serious point that Dickens

makes in this scene is that desire for wealth will make people abase themselves and betray members of their own family.

   • The enthusiasm with which the pale young gentleman mounts his pugilistic assault on Pip, despite being repeatedly knocked down, provides the humor of the encounter. Pip's reward as the victor in this chivalric tournament is the honor of kissing Estella's cheek. Dickens's point is that from the start Pip is aware that Estella's cold affection is "worth nothing" and is as much empty posturing as the pale young gentleman's boxing.

   • Too intimidated to answer Miss Havisham's questions directly to the lady herself, Joe awkwardly directs his responses to Pip. The humor of the situation is undercut by Pip's becoming ashamed of Joe when Estella's "eyes laughed mischievously." Dickens uses the scene to show how Pip is gradually being seduced to think of gentility as a virtue and of childlike simplicity as a failing.

5. Responses will vary. Students should cite Pip's external conflicts, such as struggling to gain Estella's favor and to make Joe less common. Students should mention the internal conflicts Pip has in relation to these external conflicts. For example, Pip struggles to overcome his poor self-image by deciding to educate himself and become a gentleman. He also struggles with feelings of shame and ingratitude regarding Joe.

6. Pip lacks self-confidence and selfless love. Except for Biddy and Joe, all who figure in Pip's childhood are dissatisfied in some way: Estella is dissatisfied with Pip's commonness; Miss Havisham, with the misfortune of her past; Mrs. Joe, with her family; Pip's convict, with justice; Miss Havisham's relatives, with their prospects for inheriting her estate.

7. Students should note that Pip is a prisoner of his environment and social class. He has been "jailed" by his sister's cruelties and is trapped and bullied by Mr. Pumblechook. Pip feels that his station in life—as an uneducated orphan apprenticed to a common blacksmith—bars him from genteel society. By Chapter 19, he is eager to break away from his home and village and to enter a new phase of life: to bloom as a gentleman.

8. Responses will vary. Students may view Joe as someone who lets his cranky wife pick on Pip, and someone who is not able to help Pip advance his station in life. However, Joe shows unconditional love for Pip, admires and encourages Pip, and does not begrudge him the chance to leave and try a profession other than blacksmithing.

9. Pumblechook, a hypocrite, hopes to profit from Pip's new wealth and status by outrageously trying to convince Pip that he has always been Pumblechook's "favourite fancy and . . . chosen friend." Pumblechook wants "More Capital" to expand his seed trade, and, at the very least, wants bragging rights for being "the humble instrument . . . leading up to this," that is, having recommended Pip to Miss Havisham. Pip's ironic change in attitude toward Pumblechook ("I remember feeling convinced that I had been much mistaken in him, and that he was a sensible practical good-hearted prime fellow") shows the seductive, pernicious effects of his sudden wealth; he is susceptible to the flattery of those who hope to benefit from his good fortune.

■ Reading Strategies

Cause and Effect of Pip's Expectations

Responses will vary. Sample responses follow.

Causes: Events and characters that inspire Pip's expectations include Estella's comments about his being common, his first encounter with the genteel environment while attending on Miss Havisham, his being bound to Joe in the smithy, and Mr. Jaggers's announcement of his coming into "property."

Effects: The effects of his expectations include a desire to learn to read and write and become a gentleman. His time at Satis House has left him feeling alienated from the environment from which he came and aware that he is unable to fit in at the higher social level. He is no longer comfortable with Joe and is pained by Joe's social deficiencies; these feelings cause Pip guilt.

Follow-up: Responses will vary. Possible negative effects that students may mention include the emotional and physical distance between Pip and Joe, corruption of his innocence by the allure of the things money can buy, and disappointment should he fall short of his expectations. Possible positive effects include experiencing a world beyond the village and working-class life, winning the love of Estella, fulfilling his expectations, and helping Joe rise above his station at the forge.

Chapters 20–35

■ Making Meanings

READING CHECK

a. Pip reencounters Herbert Pocket at Barnard's Inn, the living quarters which they will later share.

b. Pip's nickname is Handel.

c. Herbert knows that Miss Havisham has been rearing Estella to make men miserable.

d. Pip is not to be educated for any profession in particular. His benefactor simply wishes him to be a gentleman.

e. The convict does not recognize Pip because Pip is older, he is dressed as a gentleman, and Herbert calls him Handel.

f. Pip has no real intention of ever returning.

---

1. Responses will vary, but students will most likely define *gentleman* in terms of character traits—such as honesty, integrity, and compassion—rather than in terms of etiquette.

2. As Pip becomes more of a "gentleman," his feelings toward those who truly love him decrease in an equal proportion. He becomes haughty, adopts an extravagant lifestyle, and causes both himself and Herbert to incur debt. Nevertheless, the fact that he continues to feel guilty shows that some of the simple, loving Pip remains.

3. Pip finds the atmosphere in Mr. Jaggers's offices dismal. Students may note that dimly lit rooms, gruesome mementos, plaster busts of criminals, and scuffed and greasy walls contribute to this feeling. London and Barnard's Inn have a similar atmosphere for Pip. London is "ugly, crooked, narrow, and dirty," with a thick layer of dust and grit covering everything; the gallows where the city's condemned prisoners are hanged give Pip "a sickening idea of London." Barnard's Inn is shabby; it is shrouded in soot and smoke; it smells of "all the silent rots"; the windows are grimy and cracked.

4. Pumblechook, Herbert Pocket's father, and Mrs. Pocket all struggle with social position. Wemmick, Herbert, and Joe are at ease with their social position. Pip has his true friendships with those who are most at ease with their status.

5. Responses will vary. Students should note most or all of the following points: Estella is much more beautiful and womanly, "in all things winning admiration." She is no longer insulting, but is still proud, aloof, cold, and condescending. Pip admires Estella more than ever before, but remains easily intimidated by her and feels inferior in her presence.

6. Responses will vary. Students should note most or all of the following points: Since leaving for London, Pip has returned to the forge only once, and only because he was summoned to his sister's funeral. On his earlier visit to Satis House to see Estella, Pip intentionally stayed at an inn rather than visit with Joe—a fact that Biddy could have easily ascertained. Biddy is also aware that Pip's largess in the form of "penitential codfish" has become his preferred way of expressing affection: from a distance, both physically and emotionally. Pip's actions indicate his insecurity with his new position because he fears that association with Joe and Biddy will jeopardize his standing as a gentleman. The guilt he feels reveals his continuing sense of loyalty to them.

7. Responses will vary. Dickens is probably preparing readers for a revelation showing Estella to have some connection with crime or with some part of Pip's past.

8. *Estella* is a form of *stella,* Latin for *star,* and the character, though beautiful, is distant and cold. Havisham sounds like "Have is sham" or "Have a sham," as events in her life prove true. The Pockets' name is humorous, considering their need for money to fill their pockets because of their numerous children and Mrs. Pocket's expectations. Drummle's name is representative of his monotonous, drumming personality and his violent nature (beating drum).

9. Responses will vary. Students should note that Pip finds Newgate Prison "much neglected" and the felons poorly lodged and fed. Dickens, speaking through Pip, says that the state of the prison is an example of "public wrongdoing." It can be inferred that Dickens wanted to see prisoners treated more humanely.

10. Responses will vary. Students should note that while Wemmick is at work in Jaggers's dismal offices and among the squalor at Newgate Prison, he is dry and wooden. A man's home is his castle, though, and this is literally true for Wemmick. At home in his fanciful replica of a moated castle, he is cordial and lighthearted. Dickens is contrasting the grim, dehumanizing aspect of urban culture with the restorative nature of rural or suburban life.

■ Reading Strategies

Tracing Coincidences

Responses will vary. Sample responses follow.

1. Pip and Herbert once met and fought at Miss Havisham's.

2. Herbert felt he was being considered by Miss Havisham as a suitor for Estella.

3. The convict who gave him the two one-pound notes is on the carriage with him discussing the incident. He learns that the criminal he helped was tried for prison breaking and was given a life sentence.

4. It is this nickname that prevents Pip from being recognized on the coach by the criminal.

Follow-up: Responses will vary. Students who demand realism in a novel may object to coincidences. Others may willingly accept it as a convention of fiction.

Chapters 36–48

■ Making Meanings

READING CHECK

a. The first thing that Pip does with his yearly allowance is try to establish Herbert in business.

b. Estella plans to marry Drummle.

c. Pip is twenty-three when he learns the identity of his benefactor.

d. Pip's benefactor is "his convict," the man Pip helped on the marshes. He has been living in Australia.

e. Magwitch made his fortune honestly as a sheep farmer.

f. Pip realizes that Molly is Estella's mother.

g. Compeyson was the man to whom Miss Havisham was engaged—the man who swindled her, then canceled the wedding.

1. Responses will vary. Many students will find that Pip overreacted. Some may think him ungrateful and discourteous to Magwitch. Others may understand his reaction as shock at the unexpected and disappointing revelation.

2. Responses will vary. Students should include most or all of the following points: Both Estella and Pip spurn the affectionate touches of their benefactors. Estella and Pip's reactions are haughty, cold, and condescending—the negative qualities of being raised by Miss Havisham or educated to be a gentleman. Unlike Estella, however, Pip is moved when he sees that he has reduced Magwitch to tears.

3. Responses will vary. Students may argue that Miss Havisham wants Estella to continue to break the hearts of as many suitors as possible. It is more likely, however, that she is deeply touched by Pip's confession of love for Estella and recalls the love she once felt. Moreover, she probably realizes that Drummle is too much like Compeyson and that Estella will suffer as she did in such a match.

Students should note that Miss Havisham's objections signal a softening in her character and a realization that she, Estella, and Pip are all the victims of her obsession for revenge.

4. Miss Havisham realizes that by raising Estella to be hardhearted, cold, and aloof, she now has a daughter unable to give her love.

5. Responses will vary. Most students will think that Pip either shows a gallant, generous spirit and willingness to forgive, or has suffered an incredible lapse of memory, since Estella's scorn and contempt for Pip's clothes and manners generated his dissatisfaction with his common life in the first place and became the impetus for his dream to become a gentleman, all of which has made him extremely unhappy.

6. Responses will vary. Dickens seems to be contrasting the efforts of the uneducated, abused, humbly born Magwitch with those of the privileged but disappointed Miss Havisham. Miss Havisham was ruined by her great expectations, while Magwitch had no opportunity for such expectations and is therefore working so that Pip will have the opportunities that he himself has been denied.

7. The most obvious answer is that Molly is Estella's mother, but Dickens also must be preparing us for the identity of Estella's father; the most likely person is Magwitch.

8. Responses will vary. Students should note that Pip's concern for his patron's safety grows when he realizes he is the reason that the convict's life is in jeopardy and that he is thus responsible for Magwitch. This increasing concern signals a gradual return to the more selfless, compassionate, and loyal Pip of childhood.

9. Responses will vary. Students should note that Pip feels that a person in his position—meaning a gentleman—cannot accept money from someone like Magwitch, a convict. He also feels that it would be unseemly to take more money, considering the uncertain feelings he has toward Magwitch. Students may express the opinion that Pip's reasons are not noble, since they spring from a sense of superiority and false pride. Pip does not appreciate that Magwitch has paid society's price for his crimes, turned away from a life of crime, and earned his fortune honestly through hard work. Students may feel instead that Pip's motives are noble in that he is trying not to be a hypocrite by accepting money from a person he abhors.

10. Responses will vary. Students may think of a foundation that extends grants as a benefactor. They may also mention people who give scholarships to schools, or even those who participate in mentoring programs. Accept any answer that shows a grasp of the concept.

■ Reading Strategies

Retelling / Summarizing

Magwitch:

Experience of misfortune: He was deserted as a child and had to steal food to survive. He grew up as a drifter until he fell in with Compeyson. Compeyson led him into a life of crime, which resulted in his arrest and imprisonment. He escaped and was again imprisoned. Then, he was sent to Australia.

Reaction or result: He vowed revenge on Compeyson, but he also has earned a fortune through honest labor in Australia.

Connection to Pip: Pip is the recipient of Magwitch's fortune because of his act of kindness years ago. Magwitch aspires to make Pip a gentleman.

Pip's reaction to benefactor: Pip's reaction is horror upon learning that his benefactor is a criminal. He treats Magwitch with disdain. The shock of disappointment makes him cold to the generosity of Magwitch.

Miss Havisham

Experience of misfortune: Miss Havisham was abandoned years ago by her fiancé, Compeyson.

Reaction or result: She imprisons herself on the day which was to have been her wedding day. The clocks are stopped, the reception room is untouched except by decay, and she continues to wear her wedding dress.

Connection to Estella: Miss Havisham adopts Estella and raises her, according to Herbert, to wreak havoc on men as Miss Havisham's revenge. However, Miss Havisham also adopts Estella so that she will have someone to love.

Estella's reaction to benefactor: Estella claims she cannot love Miss Havisham because Miss Havisham never taught her how.

Follow-up: The "gentleman" criminal with which Magwitch associated is the same man who broke Miss Havisham's heart.

Chapters 49–59

■ Making Meanings

> **READING CHECK**
>
> **a.** Miss Havisham wants Pip to indicate that he has for-given her by writing "I forgive her" under her name on a sheet of paper.
>
> **b.** He saves her from a fire.
>
> **c.** Magwitch and Pip are planning to take a steamer to Hamburg or Rotterdam.
>
> **d.** A man sentenced to death forfeits his estate to the Crown.
>
> **e.** Herbert leaves for Cairo.
>
> **f.** Pip becomes a clerk.

1. Students may find his reunion with Estella an indica-tion that his greatest expectation, to marry Estella, will be realized. They may see his maturity into a gentleman as fulfillment of his expectations. Others may see Estella's request that they be "friends apart" as an indication that they will not marry, and his job in trade as falling short of expectations.

2. Responses will vary. Pip shows no false pride when he says that he feels "humbled and repent-

ant" and hopes he is worthy of Biddy. However, he remains somewhat self-centered in failing to consider that, over the years, Biddy may have become attracted to Joe's warm, loving character. Pip, after all, has neglected her for years.

3. Responses will vary. In Chapter 17, Biddy waves away Pip's declaration that he wishes he could fall in love with her; she regrets that he loves Estella, who treats him scornfully. In Chapter 18, the relationship with Joe is foreshadowed by his and Biddy's comfortable domesticity as they pre-pare to send Pip off to London. In Chapter 27, at Biddy's recommendation Joe travels to London with a message for Pip. Joe seems motivated to act on Biddy's suggestions. In Chapter 35, while Pip and Biddy discuss Joe, her concern for Joe's feelings, should Pip not visit frequently as promised, reveals a closeness between them.

4. Responses will vary. Students should note most or all of the following points: Pip now admires Magwitch's goodness and gratefully acknowl-edges him as his benefactor. That Pip will not inherit Magwitch's wealth proves that Pip's efforts to save Magwitch and his subsequent loyalty to the dying convict are not motivated by a hope for material gain. Pip's new attitude toward Magwitch, therefore, is sincere.

5. Responses will vary. Students should note most or all of the following points: Miss Havisham regrets the harm she has done to Pip and Estella and wants to atone by undoing some of the wrongs. Pip refuses Miss Havisham's money because he does not want to be self-serving. He also wants to be more self-reliant.

6. Responses will vary. Students should note most or all of the following points: The childlike Pip is reborn at the end of the novel. His hankering after money, his false pride, and his ingratitude toward Joe are gone; in their place are an eagerness to earn his own living and repay his debts, an honest humility regarding himself, and gratitude toward Joe.

7. Responses will vary. Estella's parentage is ironic because she appears to be a lady of aristocratic birth. She ridicules Pip for being common, yet if the truth were known, she would be an outcast from genteel society. At one point in the novel, Pip considers her the one thing in his life not tainted by crime.

8. Responses will vary. Students may choose Joe, who has never begrudged Pip the chance of advancement, or they may make a case for Pip himself, who uses his money to secretly establish Herbert's career.

9. True friends, such as Pip and Herbert, never let their social positions, which are constantly changing, interfere with their feelings for one another. Pip and Herbert's relationship demonstrates Dickens's conception of true love between friends; it is constant, freely given, and unmotivated by any desire to control, hurt, or use each other.

10. Responses will vary. Some students may view the present ending as happy, although ambiguous. Others will wish for a more happy, "Hollywood" ending. Accept any responses that show genuine reflection on the text.

■ Reading Strategies

Identifying Expectations

Responses may vary. Sample responses follow.

Pip aspires to be a gentleman and win Estella's love.

He succeeds in being gentlemanly in manner if not in class and wins Estella's love (though not everyone may agree that they marry).

Magwitch expects Pip to realize the dream that he, Magwitch, cannot—to be a gentleman. Some may also feel that he expects Pip's appreciation.

Magwitch dies believing he has fulfilled his goals; he is proud of who Pip has become (though he does not know that Pip will inherit none of his money), and he has just been told his daughter is alive and is a lady—

an unexpected fulfillment of his dream of genteel life.

Miss Havisham expects that Estella will carry out her plan of revenge on men. She also expects that Estella will love and appreciate the advantages she has given Estella.

For a while, Miss Havisham's expectations are met; ultimately, though, they are not—and she realizes her folly in thinking or even hoping that they could be— for she dies alone, and Estella chooses to marry a man as cruel as Compeyson.

Herbert expects to make partner in a shipping company. Because of Pip, he does so.

Estella expresses only one expectation and that is to change her life by marrying.

This she does, for she marries a cruel man.

Biddy expects to become a teacher.

She accomplishes this.

Orlick expects to pay back those he feels have slighted him in some way, namely Pip.

Though he does capture and hurt Pip, he is unsuccessful in his revenge and is ultimately arrested for his crimes against Pumblechook.

Follow-up: Jaggers becomes Pip's guardian and frequent advisor; it is through their acquaintance that Pip meets Wemmick and is able to assist Herbert in his expectations. By keeping Magwitch's secret, Jaggers assists Pip's benefactor. Jaggers provided Miss Havisham with Estella, and he kept the secret of Estella's identity. This secret ultimately creates a restless, coldhearted young woman. It is through Jaggers that Pip arranges for Orlick to be dismissed from his position as Miss Havisham's porter.

Answer Key (cont.)

Literary Elements Worksheets

■ Atmosphere

Responses will vary but should be supported by the text. Sample responses follow.

1. **Point in novel:** Pip returns from a visit to Miss Havisham's and encounters Orlick on the road (Chapter 15).

   Atmosphere: ominous

   Details/Language: It is a "very dark night," and the mist falls "wet and thick"; in the fog, everything is a "blur." Orlick is described as growling.

2. **Point in novel:** The evening of Magwitch's arrival.

   Atmosphere: gloomy, stormy

   Details/Language: It had been "stormy and wet" day after day. The wind has blown out all the lights in the hall and in the street (Chapter 39). This not only reflects how Pip feels after Estella's behavior at the ball, but also foreshadows the darkness that overcomes him when he realizes all of his expectations about his benefactor have been based on misperceptions.

3. **Point in novel:** The day Pip and Herbert plan to get Magwitch to safety.

   Atmosphere: one of anticipation

   Details/Language: The day is described as "one of those March days when the sun shines hot and the wind blows cold" (Chapter 54). The weather is mixed, just as the day's outcomes will be. Pip and his friends will be unsuccessful at saving Magwitch, but Pip realizes the extent to which he has warmed to his benefactor.

Follow-up: Answers to these questions are incorporated in the sample responses above.

■ Theme

Responses will vary, depending upon theme chosen. Sample answers follow.

1. The convict Magwitch seems to be a threat, but he protects Pip by taking responsibility for the pilfered food. Pip's experience in Satis House is, in reality, miserable, yet he concocts a fabulous story about his activities there.

2. To Pip, it appears that Miss Havisham is his benefactor. In reality, he is being supported by a convicted criminal. Pip has a false belief that if he becomes a gentleman, then Estella will approve of him.

3. Pip continues to believe that Miss Havisham is his benefactor and plans for him to marry Estella. However, Estella is making plans to marry someone else.

4. Pip is forced to search beneath the appearance of the hardened criminal and come to terms with the loyal and generous individual hidden beneath that exterior.

5. Though Pip appears to lose his station in society as a gentleman by association with Magwitch, he also realizes that Magwitch and Joe (with whom he was reluctant to associate while he was establishing himself in society) have the true disposition of a "gentleman," qualities of honesty, compassion, loyalty, and pride in work.

Follow-up: Responses should develop the chosen theme through all five sections of the novel.

■ Figurative Language

Responses may vary. Sample responses follow.

1. By Pip's saying that Mrs. Joe held his head like a boot would hold a boot-jack, he means that she held his head very tightly, as if he were in a vise. This illustrates the unaffectionate relationship between Mrs. Joe and Pip.

2. In this passage, Pip is telling us how much trouble he had with the alphabet and illustrating that it caused him emotional pain and worry.

3. The nervousness and awkwardness of Joe is made clear by how he handles a common object such as his hat as if it were fragile.

4. The image Dickens is presenting is an exaggerated one of "the Avenger" being so shaken by Pip that it was as if he were flying.

5. After Mrs. Joe's death Pip describes the illogical way that those still alive discuss the dead—as if they themselves were never going to die.

Follow-up: Responses should illustrate an understanding of the concept of simile.

■ *Bildungsroman*

Responses will vary. Sample responses follow.

Exposition/Rising Action

- Pip is confronted with Estella's estimation of him as "ignorant and backward." For the first time he considers his social standing. He learns to read and write. Pip becomes an apprentice to Joe and, after coming into property, he begins to study under Matthew Pocket. He is learning to be a gentleman.

- Pip learns the heavy burden of guilt that comes from not being honest with those you love. He comes to understand what it feels like to be considered inadequate in another's eyes. His fear of such inadequacies causes him to avoid Joe, thus incurring guilt: This is the moral dilemma he faces.

Turning Point

- Pip learns Magwitch is his benefactor. He discovers through him that Miss Havisham's fiancé was Compeyson.

- Pip's lessons are in heartache and disappointment: Estella marries Drummle, Miss Havisham has manipulated him, and his benefactor is a criminal. He learns that his expectations of who he was to become have been built on false foundations, and his dreams have crashed around him.

Falling Action/Denouement/Resolution

- Pip deduces that Molly and Magwitch are Estella's

parents. He learns the shipping trade and eventually is made a partner.

- Pip realizes that both Magwitch and Joe are (and have always been for him) gentlemen. He realizes by meeting young Pip that he can forgive himself for what he thinks was poor treatment of Joe—for clearly Joe and Biddy harbor no resentment. He comes to terms with his grandiose expectations and seems to settle into the dignity of Herbert's work.

Follow-up: Responses will vary.

■ Moral Fairy Tale

Responses may vary. Sample responses follow.

Knight: Pip: He wants to save Estella from the prison of Satis House that Miss Havisham has built around her own bitterness.

Princess: Estella: Estella fits both the positive and the negative connotations of a princess. She is lovely but remote. She is privileged but in need of a "knight."

Fairy Godmother: Some may identify Miss Havisham in this role; other students may argue that Magwitch assumes this role. They both inspire Pip to great expectations, though Miss Havisham does this under false pretenses.

Wicked Witch: Mrs. Joe: Her harsh treatment of Pip may lead students to identify her as the wicked witch. Some students may feel that Miss Havisham is a grotesque and frightening wicked witch in her decaying dress and vengeful plans.

Wise Man: Joe: Joe is consistently an example of wisdom in the novel.

Monster/Ogre: Magwitch: His frightening appearance in the cemetery at the beginning of the novel and Pip's reaction at his return indicate that Pip thinks of him this way. Orlick, who is cruel and without a conscience, also fulfills this fairy-tale element.

Castle: Wemmick's home is a miniature castle. Satis House could be compared to a castle ruin.

Treasure: The treasure for Pip is becoming a gentleman so that he can win Estella.

Follow-up

Do not assume that appearance is reality. It is in pursuit of the treasure that you gain true wealth.

- Students may mention the clock stopped at 8:40, the room at Satis House with the decaying cake, and Miss Havisham's continuing to wear her wedding dress. Wemmick's castle is fantastic and whimsical, like something from a children's story.

- Most will agree that it seems appropriate. (You may wish to read to them the original ending for this story, which is less fairy tale-like.)

Vocabulary Worksheets

If you wish to score these worksheets, assign the point values given in parentheses.

■ Vocabulary Worksheet 1

Chapters 1–19

A. *(5 points each)*

1. d. arrogantly	9. a. respected
2. c. with an uneasy feeling	10. a. mysteriously
	11. c. miserable
3. b. sympathizing with	12. b. spreading throughout
4. a. less severe	
5. d. deception	13. d. gloomy
6. b. alarm	14. c. forceful
7. c. sense of foreboding	15. a. in a showy manner
8. d. perceptively	

B. *(5 points each)*

16. – 20.
Responses will vary but students' sentences should reflect an understanding of the word through proper use in context.

■ Vocabulary Worksheet 2

Chapters 20–59

A. *(5 points each)*

1. a. joking	9. a. capped
2. d. tyrannical	10. d. mercy
3. b. authoritatively	11. c. repeated
4. b. doing without	12. a. hatred
5. c. dislike	13. d. irreverently
6. a. unerasable	14. c. almost unnoticeable
7. d. weakening	
8. b. disbelieving	15. c. offered

B. *(5 points each)*

16. b. bravery : valor
17. c. knowledgeable : ignorant
18. b. miser : selfish
19. c. compassionate : tenderness
20. a. opposition : agreement

Exploring the Connections

■ A Dickens of an Ending

> **READING CHECK**
>
> **a.** Dickens changed this original ending because Bulwer-Lytton urged him to do so.
>
> **b.** In the original ending, Drummle is killed by a horse.
>
> **c.** The two meet on a street in London; she is driving a small pony carriage.

1. Responses will vary according to personal taste. Accept all well-reasoned, well-written explanations.

2. Pip seems to be satisfied that Estella has become a caring, feeling individual, even though he recognizes that she has learned this through suffering. Pip does not seem to harbor negative feelings toward her.

3. In the original ending, Pip abandons all of his expectations, which gives a complete ending to the moral tale. In the revised ending, by hinting that Pip and Estella will not part, Dickens makes it seem that Pip's romantic expectation will be fulfilled.

4. Responses will vary according to personal opinion. Many students will reject the "Hollywood" aspects of the published ending after they read the original ending. They may feel that if Dickens originally wanted to end the novel in one way, by changing it he compromised the story as a whole. Accept answers that show thoughtful evaluation of both endings.

Connecting with the Novel

Fairy-tale endings are normally happy, as is the published conclusion. It is fantastic that Pip and Estella should happen to meet on a visit to Satis House, since neither has been there in eleven years. The setting for that reunion is rather grotesque, considering the ruined state of the property.

■ Class, Tradition, and Money

> **READING CHECK**
>
> **a.** The middle classes did clean work.
>
> **b.** Working class families were poorest when the children were small, because they were not yet earning wages and because the wife in the family could no longer work.
>
> **c.** A landed gentleman was called "Squire."

1. Responses will vary. Students will probably see that it is more likely for a person to be able to successfully raise his or her status with money today than it was in Victorian England.

2. Responses will vary. Students may see the title of "doctor" or "lawyer" as a symbol of status. Cars, clothing, and houses are all status symbols.

3. Responses will vary. Students may think that there is no aristocracy, or they may think that people with "old money" are the aristocracy. They may think that members of the computer industry are the new aristocracy, or that figures from the sports or entertainment world are members of an aristocracy. Accept answers that touch

on what students have learned about the aristocracy from the novel or the selection.

4. The middle class valued education, hard work, sexual morality, religion, family life, sobriety, thrift, ambition, punctuality, constructive use of leisure, and prudent marriage. The middle class, unlike the lower class, could afford educational opportunities but had to work hard to maintain social standing, unlike the aristocracy, who inherited their standing. The middle class resented the idleness of the upper class.

Connecting with the Novel

Answers will vary. Joe was a member of the working class; Pumblechook, Matthew Pocket, and Jaggers had low, middle, and high places in the middle class, respectively; and Miss Havisham was part of the aristocracy. Pip was a part of the working class, though he was destined to be a skilled worker, which gave him slightly higher rank. He thought he would go to London to become educated and learn a profession, but Magwitch wished for him to be a gentleman. Eventually, Pip settled happily into the middle class with an office job.

■ The Rules of the Game

> **READING CHECK**
>
> **a.** A would-be gentleman should seek the society of those above himself.
>
> **b.** The proper thing to do with your napkin was to drape it over your knee.
>
> **c.** Bits of bread should be broken off, not bitten off.

1. Responses will vary, but most students will probably recognize that setting guests at ease is more mannerly than asking them to adopt some other behavior.

2. Responses will vary.

3. The irony is that those of so-called higher social station will seek the company of those higher than themselves, not those below them in rank.

4. The 1800s were described in this way because manners and social station were what was considered important, and this attitude produced a self-conscious society. Such an emphasis likewise produced insecurity because one's reputation could be besmirched or thwarted by a "wrong" gesture or acquaintance.

Connecting with the Novel

Herbert Pocket was very gentle and encouraging in his teaching of manners to Pip and did his best to make him feel comfortable, so students will probably say that Pocket did not act as a censor. However, Pip himself acted like a censor when he was embarrassed by Joe's behavior.

■ Interior

READING CHECK

a. "Interior" refers to the internal refuge to which woman's mind has withdrawn in order to escape the pain in her heart.

b. The two characters in the poem are the mind and the heart.

1. Responses will vary. It is tragic that her heart and mind are divided and she lives in the interior of her mind, having locked out her heart.

2. Responses will vary. The tone begins as a gentle or reflective tone, but students may note that the conclusion is more fervent.

3. The rhyme scheme is *abab cdcd efef.* The rhyme scheme is neat and simple like the interior of the subject's mind.

4. The imagery of emotional pain contradicts the orderly world created in the woman's mind. Words such as "cold," "pain," and "wailing" clash with the "quiet," "narrow," and "sweet" imagery of the first two stanzas.

Connecting with the Novel

The notion of imposing order to ease a broken heart is present in both *Great Expectations* and "Interior."

Miss Havisham literally lives in a dark and "quiet . . . narrow room" and her "things are waxen near/And set in decorous lines," just as on her wedding day. As with the woman in the poem, she is bolting "the door against her heart" and living only in her mind. The subject "Interior" has mentally closed herself off, but into a lovely ordered room; Miss Havisham has stopped time at the moment of her disappointment and what was once a lovely room is now in decay.

■ Casa

READING CHECK

a. The narrator lives in both Paterson, New Jersey, and Puerto Rico.

b. The women of the family gather in Mamá's living room.

1. Responses will vary but because the experiences of Mamá's "casa" are richly detailed and warm compared to the brief, cold description of Paterson, students will probably prefer the Puerto Rican home.

2. Responses will vary, but students will probably understand from the reading that "la Loca" means "crazy."

3. Mamá and her daughters tell the stories for the benefit of the young daughters, to preserve the cultural mores and prepare the young girls to relate to men in society.

4. Mamá weaves together the ends of hair as she weaves together fact and fiction to create a story that is meant to convey some single truth. It is a bit painful—the braiding for the narrator, and the story for her young aunt. Both the storytelling and the braiding are appropriate for decent and presentable young girls.

Connecting with the Novel

Both María la Loca and Miss Havisham are women who were abandoned by their fiancés and who never moved past this moment. This is clear in Miss Havisham's forever wearing her wedding gown and in María la Loca's constant humming of the wedding march. These women were both ruined by this moment, and they serve as examples of what can happen if a woman is not careful enough in love.

■ Dick Whittington

READING CHECK

a. Dick Whittington had heard that the streets of London were paved with gold.

b. Dick Whittington paid a penny for his cat.

c. The cat was valuable because of its skill as a mouser.

---

1. Responses will vary. "Rags-to-riches" stories provide the element of hope to everyone. They make the improbable seem possible.

2. Responses will vary. The protagonist is struggling, as in most stories, and stumbles upon that which will be of value to others (his cat) and that leads to his own good fortune.

3. Dick Whittington's tenacious character is demonstrated by the fact that he sets off on his own and does not give up when things become difficult for him. He proves that he is not afraid to ask for help by asking for a ride to London and haggling for the cat, and he proves his generosity by sharing his newfound wealth even with the cook, who was rude to him.

4. The foreshadowing in the fairy tale occurs when Whittington hears the Bow Bells saying "Turn again, Whittington, Thrice Lord Mayor of London." This incident foreshadows that he will become Mayor of London.

5. Responses will vary. The moral of the fairy tale is that true success will come to those who do not let their pride get in the way of their actions.

Connecting with the Novel

Both Dick Whittington and Pip are orphans. Each sets out for London with aspirations and a desire to raise

his social station in life. Dick Whittington differs from Pip in that he does not let his pride get the better of him, even when good fortune comes his way.

■ If—

READING CHECK

a. You should trust yourself.

b. You should begin again and not speak of your loss.

c. The speaker is giving advice on how to be an admirable person.

---

1. Responses will vary.

2. Kipling personifies the experiences of triumph and disaster and the intangible quality of willpower; they are presented as characters that a person will encounter in life.

3. Responses will vary. Students may mention that triumph and disaster should be treated similarly because they are both temporary situations. Triumph and disaster are devious in that they provide a false sense of security or of insecurity.

4. Responses will vary. Students should indicate their recognition of the speaker's conditions of self-control in success; his supposition of self-confidence in distress; and his qualification of maintaining a balanced perspective regardless of events in one's life.

5. Responses will vary. Students may say that the capitalization of *man* indicates that it is an ideal, not simply a stage in the growth process. Others may note that the speaker seems to be saying *if* you behave in the manner described, then you will become an admirable person, a true gentleman or lady.

Connecting with the Novel

Responses will vary.

Pip fell short of Kipling's ideal when

• he grew tired of waiting to discover the identity of his benefactor

- he let his dream of Estella and wealth dominate his life to the point where the supposed loss of them left him feeling hollow
- he turned away from the "common touch" of Joe and Biddy to "walk with" those he thought to be gentlemen

Pip fulfilled Kipling's ideal when

- he did not resent those who had manipulated him, such as Estella and Miss Havisham
- he accepted Herbert's job offer and began a new lifestyle without complaint
- he recognized and appreciated the virtues of Joe, Magwitch, and others he had once considered common. Then he became a true gentleman.

■ The Prodigal Son

> **READING CHECK**
>
> a. He decides to return home when he realizes that servants on his father's farm fare better than he does.
>
> b. The son was going to ask to be treated as a servant.

1. Responses will vary. Students may understand and find it realistic that the reckless young man spends his money and is then too proud to return home. Some may also identify with the shame of having to return home.
2. Neither recognizes the depth of his father's love for him.
3. This parable speaks to the themes of love and appearance versus reality—the young son appears more celebrated than the elder, but this is not true. Students may say that the parable touches on the idea of great expectations that are not met, but in the end the hero realizes that the expected was always present.
4. Parables and fairy tales are told with the intent of conveying a moral. This is normally achieved after a character is brought low through his or her actions, or those of others, and then celebrated

or redeemed in the end.

Connecting with the Novel

Pip is like the prodigal son who left to claim his fortune, but after losing it was too ashamed to return home defeated. Joe shares the values of the father in the parable. He will take Pip back inspite of his prideful sins, because he loves unconditionally.

■ You must know that I do not love

> **READING CHECK**
>
> The speaker does not love yet in order to love in the future.

1. Responses will vary. Unrequited love is a common theme in literature because of the passionate feelings it evokes, and because it is a theme to which it is easy to relate.
2. The speaker's feelings are intense and volatile, as indicated by the image of fire and cold.
3. "I love you" or "I do not love you" are the keys that the speaker holds. Saying either of these could open a "future joy" or "a wretched, muddled fate." That unknown future seems to frighten the speaker.
4. In the final stanza, the speaker admits that he or she loves "when I do not love you . . . and when I do."

Connecting with the Novel

The confusion over love expressed in the poem is reminiscent of Estella and Pip's relationship. Estella tells Pip that she cannot love but also admits to him that he is the only man she does not seek to deceive or entrap. For Pip, loving or not loving Estella is the key to a "future joy" or "a wretched, muddled fate."

Test

■ Part I

A.

1. o	**6.** l	**11.** j
2. f	**7.** m	**12.** h
3. b	**8.** e	**13.** c
4. n	**9.** k	**14.** g
5. d	**10.** a	**15.** i

B.

16. F	**21.** F
17. T	**22.** F
18. F	**23.** F
19. F	**24.** T
20. T	**25.** F

■ Part II

26. Pip meets Magwitch when Pip is seven. The escaped convict comes upon him in the cemetery and demands food and a means of filing off his leg iron. He is in debt to Pip for supplying these things.

27. Joe is married to Pip's older sister, who has raised Pip "by hand." Pip feels close to Joe, who is kind, but lives in constant fear of his sister.

28. Pip begins to worry about his status on his first trip to Satis House.

29. Miss Havisham wears her wedding dress all the time because that is what she was wearing when she received Compeyson's letter calling off the wedding. She effectively stopped her normal life at that moment.

30. Wemmick is both the practical, no-nonsense assistant to Jaggers, and the compassionate and romantic man who has built himself a "Castle" where he cares for his elderly, deaf father.

31. Students should mention two of the following: As conditions of receiving his fortune, Pip must continue to use the name "Pip," he must never try to discover the identity of his benefactor, and he must go to London to be schooled.

32. Wemmick discovers that Pip is under Compeyson's surveillance, so he sends Pip a note telling him to stay away while Herbert moves Magwitch to another apartment.

33. Miss Havisham becomes cross when Estella resists her embraces. Estella says she is exactly the woman Miss Havisham has taught her to be, which is one incapable of loving anyone, even her mother.

34. Magwitch and Molly are Estella's parents. After Miss Havisham is jilted by Compeyson, she asks Jaggers to find her a child to raise. Not long after this request, Jaggers represents Molly in her trial for the murder. He arranges for Molly's child, who is believed to be dead, to be adopted by Miss Havisham.

35. Pip was very ill and he was going to be arrested for debt, but Joe pays his debts for him.

■ Part III

a. Responses will vary. Pip originally thinks that the purpose of education is to make a person less common and coarse and thereby raise him to a higher social station in life—in short, to make him better than those without education. By the end of the novel, Pip learns that an educated person is not necessarily a morally or socially superior person and that hard work is more important than education in acquiring financial security.

b. Responses will vary. The convict's early willingness to confess to stealing the food and the file in order to save Pip from blame, the mysterious gift of the two one-pound notes, or Pip's overhearing the conversation of the man that gave him the money years later foreshadow that Magwitch is Pip's benefactor. Orlick's threatening behavior toward Pip while he is an apprentice at the forge foreshadows his later attempt on Pip's life. After meeting Molly, Pip begins to see a shadow of something familiar in Estella's face, foreshadowing Pip's discovery of their relationship. Biddy's protectiveness toward Joe's feelings regarding Pip, her understanding of his pride in working at the forge, and her lack of interest in Pip's comments about their possible compatibility foreshadow her eventual marriage to Joe.

c. Responses will vary. Students should be able to uncover many links between the novel and fairy-tale motifs in *Great Expectations*. Taken out of a fairy-tale context, most of the novel's many coincidences would be entirely unbelievable—Orlick's finding of Magwitch's discarded leg iron, for example, or the fact that Pip's benefactor is Estella's father and has connections with both Estella's adopted mother's lawyer and her former fiancé. Moreover, many characters resemble types from fairy tales: Miss Havisham is like a gingerbread-house witch who devours children; Mrs. Joe behaves like Cinderella's stepmother; Compeyson appears as a larger-than-life villain in the way he controls an insidious network of minions; Magwitch (magnanimous witch) is Pip's fairy godfather; slouching Orlick is an ogre; Estella is the beautiful princess; and Pip is the coarse and common frog granted a wish and magically transformed into a gentleman prince. Dickens's settings, too, often evoke those of fairy tales: Satis House is entirely fantastic in its dungeonlike details, and Wemmick's Gothic castle is humorously whimsical.

Students may argue that such motifs either add to the novel or detract from it. They should realize, however, that the parallels add to the depth and richness of the narrative by adding an archetypal level to the realistic social one.

d. Responses will vary. Dickens depicts English law as harsh and unyielding. Although Magwitch has atoned for his crimes, reformed himself, and become a successful and honest businessman, the law refuses to see him as anything other than a scourge to society. This attitude is as much a result of social prejudice as it is of the Crown's responsibility to maintain social order. Dickens reveals these prejudices in several ways. The coarse and common Magwitch receives a harsher sentence than the "gentleman" Compeyson; the Australian colonists look down on the transported convict who becomes more successful than they; Pip recoils when Magwitch reveals himself and he looks upon Magwitch's money as tainted by crime. Dickens also embeds an illusion to victimization in Magwitch's name—Abel, who was murdered by his brother.

e. Responses will vary. Miss Havisham eventually realizes the wrong she has done both in making Estella the instrument of her revenge against all men and in causing Pip pain. She tries to atone by offering Pip financial help (which he refuses) and by secretly financing Herbert's partnership.

f. Responses will vary according to class interaction with the Connections selection but should include a connection mentioned in the **Introducing the Connections** chart in the Study Guide.

Notes

Notes

Notes

Notes

Notes